KIFFIN, KNOLLYS AND KEACH

KIFFIN, KNOLLYS AND KEACH — REDISCOVERING OUR ENGLISH BAPTIST HERITAGE

Michael A. G. Haykin

1996

A Carey Title
published by

REFORMATION TODAY TRUST
75 Woodhill Road
Leeds LS16 7BZ
England

A Carey Title
published by
REFORMATION TODAY TRUST
75 Woodhill Road
Leeds LS16 7BZ
England

First printed 1996

ISBN 0 9527913 0 7

Distributed by
Evangelical Press
12 Wooler Street
Darlington
Co. Durham DL1 1RQ
England

Printed in Great Britain by The Bath Press, Somerset

To
William E. Payne,
a beloved brother,
who has helped to make the heritage
of the seventeenth-century English Calvinistic Baptists
a living reality for the late twentieth century

All mankind naturally were alike dry and barren, as a wilderness, and brought forth no good fruit. But God hath separated some of this barren ground, to make lovely gardens for himself to walk and delight in.

Benjamin Keach

Contents

Foreword

In this fine work Professor Michael Haykin introduces us to some of the outstanding Particular or Calvinistic Baptist leaders of the seventeenth century. They were pioneers whose work was to apply the Reformers' recovery of the gospel in a Baptist church context. They not only gave leadership to the London Particular Baptists but also exercised a significant influence throughout England. Sadly they are almost unknown to many who now delight in the truths they proclaimed. This is a book which therefore needed to be written.

The teaching of William Kiffin, Hanserd Knollys and Benjamin Keach is reflected in the *1689 Baptist Confession*. Professor Haykin summarises the teaching and significance of this Confession and also discusses its relation to the earlier *1644 Confession*. We see how these pioneers fought against great odds to establish a Baptist church order and to maintain a biblical presentation of the gospel. They were unashamedly Calvinist and thereby stood in the great Reformed tradition, but they were not Hyper-Calvinist and in fact warned against that tendency which was to undermine gospel preaching and also prove to be a By-path Meadow which was to entice so many into Doubting Castle. They also had to take a stand against Seekers and Quakers and in so doing provide their twentieth-century successors with significant warnings against the charms of the charismatic movement.

During the second half of the twentieth century there has been an important recovery of Reformation teaching among Baptists throughout the world. Significant in that recovery was the republication in 1959 of the *Baptist Confession of 1689*. After a century of neglect it has become the focus of new interest and is now in print in more languages than at any time in its history. For members of such churches this book is of fundamental importance. Other Baptists who have not subscribed to a Reformed Confession may discover that their debt to these men of the seventeenth century is greater than they ever guessed.

Robert W. Oliver
Bradford on Avon
November 1995

THE REVᴰ Mᴿ HENRY JESSEY

Henry Jessey

Introduction

The Calvinistic Baptist heritage from the seventeenth century is a sorely neglected treasure. Of the various Baptist leaders from that era, only one is well known today: John Bunyan, the "immortal dreamer". Yet, interestingly enough, he was a relatively minor player in the advance of the Baptist cause during the seventeenth century. On the other hand, men like William Kiffin, Hanserd Knollys and Benjamin Keach, who were instrumental in putting the Calvinistic Baptist cause on the map, are today complete unknowns. As this book argues, these three men have much to teach contemporary Baptists. It was Kiffin, for example, in concert with a handful of other Baptist leaders, who drew up the first *London Confession of Faith,* which laid the foundation upon which the Baptists evangelised and built churches during the tumultuous 1640s and 1650s. In fact, the conception of the church that is set forth in this *Confession* is one that is still attractive despite the passage of time and lies at the heart of vibrant Baptist witness today. Another area in which these Baptists can help their present-day descendants is with regard to the challenges posed by contemporary charismatic movements. Baptists in the seventeenth century also had to contend with such groups. In their case, it was those known to history as the Seekers and the Quakers. The way in which a Baptist leader like Knollys argued against Seeker views can be an encouragement to modern Baptists who have to give an answer to present-day charismatic claims and experiences.

Yet, seventeenth-century Baptist history is also a treasure that should be valued by all the people of God. For instance, it is Keach who pioneered the introduction of hymn-singing to Anglophone Christianity. As a hymn-writer Keach left much to be desired, but as an apologist for the practice of hymn-singing he was brilliant and the impact of his arguments is obviously still being felt today.

To delight in one's spiritual heritage, it should being noted, is not to be sectarian. I was raised a Roman Catholic in the days before

Vatican II. One of the teachings of the pre-Vatican II Roman
Catholic Church was that "outside of the church [i.e. the Roman
Catholic Church], there is no salvation". I can still recall my shock
when I was told by a third-generation Baptist, shortly after I had
become a Christian in 1974, that the human population of heaven
would consist solely of those who in this life had been Baptists! I was
appalled by the narrow-mindedness of this Baptist version of
Roman Catholic exclusiveness. Upon further reflection, I have
come to see that the spirit behind such a statement is completely
lacking in the fragrant humility of our Lord Jesus, who encouraged
his disciples to find their joy not in the fact that they belonged to a
certain denominational structure, but in the simple fact that their
"names are written in heaven" (Luke 10:20). The church of God, I
delight to confess, is far broader than those who go by the name of
Baptist.

On the other hand, as I have spent a considerable amount of time
studying Baptist history over the past eight or so years, especially
that of the Calvinistic Baptists, I have come to see that this heritage
is something that needs to be first rediscovered and then cherished.
Yes, the Christian family is broader than the Baptist community, but
that does not mean that the Baptist tradition is not worthy of study
and reflection. I am convinced that historical Baptist convictions are
fully biblical ones and that the Baptist heritage has much to teach
both those who are Baptists and those believers who are in other
Christian traditions. Some words of that great nineteenth-century
Baptist, C. H. Spurgeon (1834-1892), well sum up my convictions
in this regard. On the one-hundredth anniversary of the birth of
William Carey (1761-1834), the Victorian preacher could say of
Carey: "I admire Carey ... for being a Baptist: he had none of the
false charity which might prompt some to conceal their belief for
fear of offending others; but at the same time he was a man who
loved all who loved the Lord Jesus Christ."[1] It is in the spirit of these
words of Spurgeon that the following studies are offered.

It should be noted that this book does not attempt to provide an
exhaustive, consecutive history of the Baptists in the seventeenth
century. Rather, after touching on the question of Baptist origins, the
chapters in this book are focused on three key leaders and two
central documents in the first century of the Calvinistic Baptist
movement. As such there is sometimes overlap between the various
chapters. The studies seek to awaken interest in this vital, formative

period of Calvinistic Baptist history and thus further the rediscovery and appropriation of the enduring aspects of the heritage of this era.

For help in preparing the substance of Chapters 3, 6 and 7 I am indebted to Dr. Robert W. Oliver for making available to me a copy of his unpublished paper "Baptist Confession Making 1644 and 1689", which he presented to the Strict Baptist Historical Society in March, 1989. I would also like to thank Robert for writing the "Foreword" to this book. I have deeply appreciated his support and friendship over the last few years. The material in Chapters 3, 6 and 7 has already appeared in *Reformation Canada*, 13, No.4 (1990); 14, No.1 (1991); and 14, No.2 (1991). I would like to thank the editor of this journal, Rev. William Payne, for allowing me to include it here. Much of Chapter 5 first appeared in an article entitled "Hanserd Knollys (*ca.* 1599-1691) on the Gifts of the Spirit", which was published in *The Westminster Theological Journal*, 54 (1992). I wish to thank the editor of this journal, Dr Moisés Silva, for permission to include portions of this article in this book. A copy of James Barry Vaughn's unpublished PhD. thesis, "Public Worship and Practical Theology in the Work of Benjamin Keach (1640-1704)" (University of St. Andrews, 1989), was very helpful in writing what is Chapter 8 on Benjamin Keach and I want to thank Dr. Vaughn for sending me a copy of his thesis. For permission to use the portrait of Benjamin Keach on the front cover, Dr. Peter Masters and the Metropolitan Tabernacle, London, England are warmly thanked. I am also indebted to Rev. Erroll Hulse for advice on the structure of the book and for his warm encouragement to publish it. Jamie Good is also thanked for the chart on the development of seventeenth-century Dissent.

October, 1995
Dundas, Ontario

The Development of Seventeenth-Century Dissent

[adapted from Michael Watts, The Dissenters (Oxford: Clarendon Press, 1978),6]

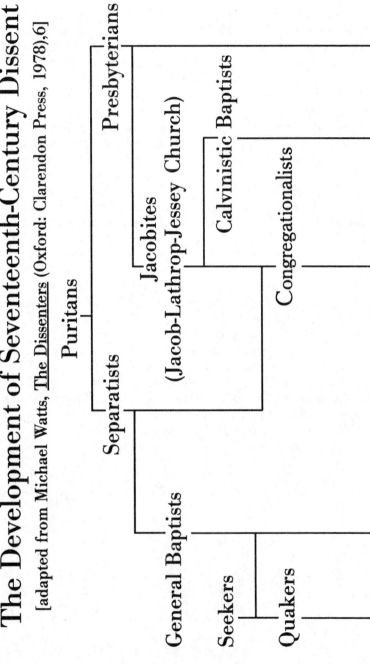

1.
The Question of Baptist Origins

Baptist successionism

There are at least three different perspectives on Baptist origins. One position, which may be called "Baptist successionism", argues for an organic succession of Baptist churches going all the way back to either the ministry of John the Baptist on the banks of the Jordan river or the day of Pentecost. "It traces a succession to the modern Baptist denomination[s] through groups of various names [such as the Paulicians, Albigensians, Waldensians]..., claiming that each group held to basic Baptist beliefs."[1] According to those who have advocated this view, it was felt to be a logical consequence of Jesus' words in Matthew 16:18: "I will build my church, and the gates of Hades shall not prevail against it." The term "church" in this verse was understood to be a reference to a local church of believers that was similar in kind to those found in modern Baptist groups. Since Christ had promised that such local churches would always be in existence throughout history, it would be questioning Jesus' integrity to believe otherwise. It was therefore incumbent upon the Baptist historian to find them in the historical record. This view has been defended by, among others, G. H. Orchard in his *A Concise History of Foreign Baptists* (1855), J. M. Cramp's *Baptist History* (1868), and J. M. Carroll in *The Trail of Blood* (1931).

It is noteworthy that this view became popular in the nineteenth century, and is not to be found in the writings of Baptists of the seventeenth and eighteenth centuries. The earliest Baptist historian, for instance, Thomas Crosby (*ca.* 1683-*ca.* 1752), in his four-volume *The History of the English Baptists* (1738-1740) does outline what might be described as a "spiritual succession" when he traces the rejection of infant baptism back to the first century. But he makes no attempt to graft all of the groups who refused to baptise infants into a kind of Baptist family tree.[2] Crosby's position is typical of other seventeenth and eighteenth-century Baptist authors who were content to affirm that there have always been, in the history of the church, faithful believers in the Lord Jesus. As W. Morgan Patterson puts it: "The writers of this early period in Baptist history apparently affirmed nothing more than a continuity of the evangelical witness."[3] The *Second London Confession of Faith* 26.3 sums up this view well when it states: "The purest Churches under heaven are subject to mixture, and error; and some have so degenerated as to become no Churches of Christ, but Synagogues of Satan; nevertheless Christ always hath had, and ever shall a Kingdom in this world, to the end thereof, of such as believe in him, and make profession of his Name."[4]

Now, the major problem with the successionist view of Baptist origins is that it simply will not pass the scrutiny of historical examination. While the groups that are claimed by these historians to be genuine Baptists often have some similarities with later Baptists, other major differences invalidate the entire thesis.[5]

The English Baptists and the Anabaptists

A second position argues that Baptist origins should be traced back to the sixteenth-century Anabaptist movement on the European continent and its offshoots in England. At the time of the Reformation, a number of the individuals who left the Roman Church refused to identify themselves with what some have called the Magisterial Reformers and the groups associated with them, that is, Martin Luther (1483-1546) in Saxony, and Ulrich Zwingli (1484-1531) and John Calvin (1509-1564) in Switzerland. These individuals by and large rejected the idea of a national church, to which every individual in the state belonged, along with its support of infant baptism. Instead, they advocated churches composed solely of believers who were admitted on the basis of a personal confession of faith and believer's baptism. Two specially prominent Anabaptists were Jakob Hutter (d. 1536), who organised what became the early Hutterite community, and Menno Simons (1496-1559), one of the founding fathers of the Mennonites.

It is interesting to note that these Anabaptists generally baptised by pouring or sprinkling. The first Anabaptist baptism took place in Zürich in January, 1525, when Conrad Grebel (*ca.* 1498-1526) baptized Jörg [George] Blaurock (*ca.* 1492-1529) by pouring water over his head, that is, by affusion. Even though a month later Grebel did baptise a certain Wolfgang Ulimann by immersion, this was exceptional; the usual mode of baptism among the Swiss Anabaptists was affusion. The early German Anabaptists, of whom Hans Hut (d.1527) is a good example, also baptised by affusion. Speaking of Hut's way of baptising believers, Rollin Stely Armour states: "Often ... Hut seems simply to have poured [water] over the person's head. Ordinarily the candidate would kneel, and others present did the same." On occasion, Hut baptised believers by dipping his thumb "in a dish of water and making a cross on the baptisand's forehead," in accordance with his view that the seal mentioned in Revelation 7:3 was baptism.[6] Menno Simons also taught and practised baptism by affusion. In fact, Simons can actually speak of baptism as "receiving a handful of water".[7]

This perspective which regards the continental Anabaptists as the forebears of the Baptists may be described as the "Anabaptist kinship" thesis. That Anabaptists were active in England prior to the clear emergence of the Baptists is demonstrable.[8] But this does not mean that there was a direct influence by these Anabaptists on the Baptists who emerged in the seventeenth century. First, it was quite possible for both groups to reach independently the identical conclusions, since both groups appealed to the Scriptures as the standard for church life and order.[9] Second, if the Baptists were deeply indebted to the Anabaptists, they would have been reluctant to admit it, due to the popular image of "Anabaptists" as violent social revolutionaries that had developed during the sixteenth century. Much of this negative image of the Anabaptists had derived from the seizure of the town of Münster in Germany by a fanatical group of Anabaptists who believed that the kingdom of God could be set up by force of arms. From 1534-1535 the inhabitants of the town were ruled by Jan Matthys and Jan Bockelson, also known as John of Leyden, who established a theocracy in which all property was held in common, polygamy legalised and adultery punished with death. Although this Anabaptist experiment was short-lived - the town fell to a Catholic army in June 1535 - and hardly representative of the main thrust of Anabaptism, the scandalous horror of Münster made the name of Anabaptist a byword for fanaticism and violent anarchy well into the seventeenth century. For example, when the first Calvinistic Baptist churches issued a Confession of faith in 1644 that outlined their theological beliefs, they stated on the title-page of the Confession that they were "commonly (though falsely) called Anabaptists".[10] They clearly wanted to dissociate themselves totally from the spectre of Anabaptism. It is thus virtually "impossible to measure the impact of Anabaptists in a situation where their impact is bound to be denied or ignored".[11] Third, in the development of the English Separatists, who had emerged from the Puritan movement of the late 1500s and who are briefly examined below, there exists a plausible explanation for the development of Baptist convictions and ideas.[12] As English Baptist historian Barrie R. White has maintained, when an explanation for the emergence of Baptist convictions from the English context of the Puritan-Separatist movement is readily available, the onus of proof lies upon those who argue for continental Anabaptism as having a decisive role in the emergence of the Baptists.[13]

Puritan-Separatist roots

The third position, which may be described as the "Puritan-Separatist Descent" view, maintains that the Baptists emerged from the matrix of the English Puritan and Separatist movements of the late sixteenth to the mid-seventeenth centuries. This view came into its own at the end of the last century for a variety of reasons, not the least of which is that it best fits and explains the historical evidence. Leading proponents include Champlin Burrage, W. T. Whitley, J. H. Shakespeare, and more recently, B. R. White. The Puritan-Separatist thesis has not, of course, gone unchallenged. It has been notably rejected by E. A. Payne, who was for many years the recognised leader of British Baptist historians.

Reformation had come to England during the reign of Henry VIII (r. 1509-1547); but it was not until the reign of his son Edward VI (r. 1547-1553) and that of his daughter Elizabeth I (r. 1559-1603) that it got a firm footing. In fact, after Elizabeth I ascended the throne there was no doubt that England was firmly in the Protestant orbit. The question that arose, though, was to what extent the Elizabethan church would be reformed. It soon become clear that Elizabeth was content with a church that was "Calvinistic in theology, [but] Erastian in Church order and government [i.e. the state was ascendant over the church in these areas], and largely mediaeval in liturgy".[14] In response to this ecclesiastical "settledness", there arose the Puritan movement, which sought to reform the Elizabethan church after the model of the churches in Protestant Switzerland, especially those in Geneva and Zürich.

Eventually, some radical Puritans, despairing of reformation within the Church of England, began to separate from the state church and organise their own Separatist congregations. The "clarion-call" of the Separatist movement was *A Treatise of Reformation without Tarrying for Anie* (1582) by Robert Browne (*ca.* 1550-1633) - "Trouble church" Browne, as one of his opponents nicknamed him.[15] Browne came from a family of substance and was related to Robert Cecil, Lord Burleigh, Elizabeth I's Lord Treasurer and chief minister. During his undergraduate years at Cambridge University, Browne had become a "thorough-going Presbyterian Puritan". Within a few years, though, he had come to the conviction that each local congregation had the right, indeed the responsibility, to elect its own elders.[16] And by 1581 he was of the opinion that the establishment of congregations apart from the Established Church and its parish churches was a necessity for, he wrote that year, "God will receive none to communion and covenant with him, which as yet are at one with the wicked."[17] That same year he established a Separatist congregation at Norwich. Experiencing persecution he and his Norwich congregation left England the following year for the freedom of the Netherlands. What attracted the Separatists to the Netherlands was its geographical proximity to England, its policy of religious toleration, its phenomenal commercial prosperity - the early seventeenth century witnessed such a flowering of Dutch literary, scientific and artistic achievement that this period has often been called "the golden age of the Netherlands" - and the Reformed nature of its churches. It was there that he published his *Treatise of Reformation*. In this influential tract, Browne set forth his views which, over the course of the next century, would become common property of all the theological children of the English Separatists, including the Baptists.

First of all, Browne willingly conceded the right of civil authorities to rule and to govern. However, he drew a distinct line between their powers in society at large and their power with regard to local churches. As citizens of the state the individual members of these churches were to be subject to civil authorities, but, he rightly emphasised, these authorities had no right "to compel religion, to plant Churches by power, and to force a submission to ecclesiastical government by laws and penalties".[18] Then, Browne conceived of the local church as a "gathered" church, that is, a company of

Christians who had covenanted together to live under the rule of
Christ, the Risen Lord, whose will was made known through his
Word and his Spirit. Finally, the pastors and elders of the church,
though they ultimately received their authority and office from God,
were to be appointed to their office by "due consent and agreement
of the church ... according to the number of the most which agree".[19]
Browne had seen clearly that the kingdom of God cannot be brought
about by the decrees of state authorities and that ultimately
Christianity is "a matter of private conscience rather than public
order, that the church is a fellowship of believers rather than an army
of pressed men" and women.[20]

Although Browne later recanted these views, he had started a
movement that could not be held in check. Browne's mantle fell to
three men - John Greenwood (*ca.* 1560-1593), Henry Barrow (*ca.*
1550-1593) and John Penry (1559-1593) - all of whom were hanged
in 1593 for what was regarded by the state as an act of civil
disobedience, namely secession from the Established Church.
However, their preaching and writings had led a significant number
in the English capital, London, to adopt Separatist principles. As
White has noted: "For many it was but a short step from impatient
Puritanism within the established Church to convinced Separatism
outside it."[21]

Now, Penry had emphasised to the state authorities that
"imprisonment, judgments, yea, death itself, are not meet weapons
to convince men's consciences, grounded on the word of God."[22]
The state and ecclesiastical authorities seem to have come to a
similar conviction, for in April 1593 a law was passed that required
everyone over the age of sixteen to attend their local parish church.
Failure to do so for an entire month meant imprisonment. If, after
three months following the individual's release from prison, he or
she still refused to conform, the person was to be given a choice of
exile or death. In other words, the Elizabethan church and state was
hoping to rid itself of the Separatist problem by sending those who
were recalcitrant into exile. Understandably, when faced with a
choice of death or exile, most Separatists chose the latter. About
forty of them ended up in Amsterdam, where they were later joined
by their pastor, a former Puritan named Francis Johnson (d. 1617).

It is noteworthy that Francis Johnson had been arrested at the
same time as Greenwood and Barrow. Though they were executed,
he was kept in prison till 1597, when he was released on the

condition that he go into exile in Canada! Needless to say, Johnson did not end up in Canada, but in Amsterdam, where his Separatist congregation was residing. Though the Separatists now had freedom to worship, their troubles were not at an end. First, Francis' brother George Johnson began to cause problems for the congregation. George began to voice complaints about his sister-in-law: her expensive clothing, her use of whalebones in her petticoats so that, according to George, she was hindered in bearing children, the fact that she stayed in bed till nine o'clock on Sunday mornings![23] To such criticisms, George added one considerably more substantial: his brother was power-hungry, and he was the centre of power, not the congregation.[24] The congregation, though, sided with Francis Johnson and his wife, and George Johnson, when he refused to withdraw his charges, was excommunicated around 1599/1600. But the troubles of this congregation were not over. In 1608 there arrived in Amsterdam another Separatist congregation led by a man named John Smyth (*ca.* 1570-1612). Initially, there was obviously a considerable amount of unanimity between the two congregations - they were both Separatist in theology and both composed of expatriate English men and women - but within a year there were significant differences between the two groups, differences that eventually led the Smyth congregation to become the first English-speaking Baptists.

John Smyth and the General Baptists

John Smyth's exact origins are unknown, though he may well have grown up at Sturton-le-Steeple in Nottinghamshire.[25] Our first definite sight of Smyth is when he was at Christ's College, Cambridge, where he obtained a B. A. in 1590 and an M. A. three years later. During this period Cambridge University was a nursery of Puritanism, and among Smyth's tutors was Francis Johnson. It is not surprising, therefore, to find Smyth in trouble for his Puritan views a few years after his departure from Cambridge. He had been ordained as a minister in the Church of England in 1594, but within three years he was voicing strong disagreement with certain aspects of that Church's liturgy. Appointed lecturer in the town of Lincoln by its Puritan-leaning town council in 1600, he stayed in this position till 1602. Some sermons that he gave at this time - later published as *The Bright Morning Starre* (1603) and *A Paterne of*

True Prayer (1605) - show a man who was Puritan in theology, but who, nevertheless, still considered himself to be a loyal member of the Church of England.[26]

By the autumn of 1607, however, Smyth had definitely become convinced of the rectitude of the Separatist position and had gathered a Separatist congregation in the town of Gainsborough in Lincolnshire on the Nottinghamshire border. It would appear that the critical factor in convincing Smyth that he should leave the Church of England was the promulgation in late 1604 of a series of church decrees by the King, James I (r. 1603-1625), requiring complete conformity of all Church of England ministers to the Thirty-Nine Articles (the doctrinal foundation of the Church of England), the *Book of Common Prayer* (which set forth the worship and liturgy of the Church of England), and acquiescence to Episcopal church government. Smyth apparently met with a number of other Puritans, including John Robinson (1575-1625) and John "Decalogue" Dod, to discuss what course of action they should take. Most decided to remain within the bosom of the Established Church. Smyth and Robinson, though, were convinced that they had to leave, for, in their view, the Church of England was beyond hope of reform.

During the course of 1607 and 1608, the Smyth congregation was harassed by the state, and the congregation made the difficult decision to leave England for the free winds of Amsterdam, Holland. Established in Amsterdam, they naturally looked for fellowship with the other English Separatist congregation in the city, that pastored by Francis Johnson. Soon, though, differences began to appear between the two congregations. In a book that Smyth published in the year of his arrival in the Netherlands, *The Differences of the Churches of the Separation* (1608), he outlined a number of areas of disagreement between his congregation and that of Johnson.[27] The most significant of these differences had to do with church government. In the Johnson congregation, there was a pastor - responsible for preaching, discipline, and leading the congregation in the observance of the sacraments - a teacher, who simply taught, and two ruling elders, who helped the pastor with the exercise of discipline. This differentiation of leadership had its roots in John Calvin's understanding of the church officers listed in Ephesians 4:11. Smyth, however, believed that pastors, teachers and elders were actually indistinguishable, and that every congregation should have a plurality of these officers.

The net result of these differences was a rupture of fellowship between the two congregations as well as a split in the Smyth congregation. John Robinson and about one hundred members found that they could not agree with the direction in which Smyth was moving, and they separated from Smyth and actually relocated in Leiden.[28] From Leiden, Robinson's congregation would eventually sail to America, landing at Plymouth in south-eastern Massachusetts in 1620. Thus, Smyth's congregation now numbered about fifty members, about a third of its original size.

In 1609, Smyth's thinking took another significant step, as he came to accept believer's baptism. The issue of baptism had been something of an embarrassment to the Separatists. According to their thinking, the Church of England was a false church. Yet, all of them had been baptised as infants by this church. Was not the efficacy of their baptism in doubt, therefore? The Separatists, though, shrank from asking, let alone answering, this question. The events associated with the revolutionary Anabaptists of Münster were still etched firmly in the memory of European Christians: believer's baptism could only lead to social and political disorder.[29] But where others feared to tread, Smyth, ever the independent thinker, forged ahead. If, he reasoned, the Church of England is not a true church, then neither is her baptism a true baptism.

Moreover, as he studied the Scriptures, he came to see that the New Testament knew only of believer's baptism and nothing of infant baptism. He outlined his new position in a treatise entitled *The Character of the Beast*, which was published in 1609. Baptism, Smyth argued, typifies the baptism with the Spirit and follows upon one's verbal confession of Christ; but infants cannot receive the baptism of the Spirit, nor can they confess Christ with their mouths. Nor are infants capable of repentance, which again must precede baptism.[30] Thus, Smyth concluded that the practice of infant baptism among the Separatists tarred them with the same brush of "heresy" as Rome and the Established Church in England: "Be it known therefore to all the Separation that we account them in respect of their constitution to be as very an harlot as either her mother England, or her grandmother Rome is, out of whose loins she came. The Separation, the youngest & fairest daughter of Rome, is an harlot; for as is the mother, so is the daughter."[31]

Smyth thus felt that he and his congregation were surrounded by a sea of apostasy. He recognised that he needed to be baptised, but in such a situation of total apostasy he felt that there was no one to whom he could turn for a proper baptism. He thus took the radical - and to his contemporaries, rightly shocking - step of baptizing himself and then baptizing his congregation.[32]

In the controversy that followed this step by the Smyth congregation, Smyth was asked by his Separatist contemporaries how he could take such a step, for if self-baptism were permissible, then churches could be established of solitary men and women, which was ridiculous. Smyth's response was that "there was no church to whom we could join with a good conscience to have baptism from them".[33] But, Smyth's critics pointed out, there was in the Netherlands a Mennonite group known as the Waterlanders, from whom he could have received baptism. Smyth thus decided to approach the Waterlanders to investigate where they stood theologically.

By this point, Smyth had also abandoned Calvinism and had adopted the views of the Dutch theologian Jacob Arminius (1560-1609), in particular the belief that Christ died for all men and women. Arminius' theological position was being heavily debated at the time in the Netherlands, and it is therefore quite understandable how Smyth came under the influence of this position.[34] From the vantage-point of his newly-adopted Arminianism, the Waterlanders were orthodox, and Smyth now came to regard his self-baptism as a premature and hasty step. Thus, together with forty-two other members of his congregation, he applied to join the Waterlander Mennonite church. This meant another baptism at the hands of the Waterlanders, and consequently an admission on the part of the Smyth congregation that their baptism by Smyth was invalid. But there were some in the Smyth congregation who refused to admit that their baptism was invalid. Led by Thomas Helwys (d. *ca.* 1615), they refused to be absorbed into the Waterlander church, and instead decided in 1612 to return to England. Smyth died the same year and his congregation, eventually received into the Waterlander church, was ultimately assimilated into Dutch Anabaptist culture.[35]

The Helwys congregation retained the Arminianism that they had adopted under Smyth's leadership, and thus became known as General Baptists, i.e. Baptists who believed in a general rather than a particular redemption. Helwys was thrown into jail almost as soon as the congregation returned to England, where he died around 1615. Helwys' small congregation - which must have consisted of no more than ten or so members when they first returned to England - survived their leader's imprisonment and death, and eventually became the General Baptist denomination. By 1626 they had established congregations in London, Coventry, Lincoln, Salisbury, and Tiverton, with roughly 150 members.[36]

The General Baptists thus clearly emerged from the womb of Puritanism and the Separatist movement. Yet, although they are the first English-speaking Baptists, it is the Calvinistic Baptists who were to become the leading Baptist denomination in the next couple of centuries. To the story of their origins we now turn.

2.
The Calvinistic Baptists

When it comes to Baptist origins in the seventeenth century, the attention of Baptist historians has largely been focused on the General Baptists. Yet, it is the Calvinistic Baptists, who, though they appear on the scene of history later than the General Baptists, are more important for the ongoing stream of Baptist history. Glen H. Stassen has enunciated four substantial reasons why he believes the spotlight should shift to the Calvinistic Baptists.[1] The General Baptists, apart from a few congregations, generally died out in the late eighteenth century in the wasteland of Unitarianism. In the early eighteenth century they had refused to censure the views of Matthew Caffyn (1628-1714), a General Baptist pastor who, finding his mind unable to fathom the mystery of the Trinity and that of the deity of Christ, concluded that neither could be true. By the mid-eighteenth century, Caffyn's way of reasoning was that of the majority of the General Baptists. As Dan Taylor (1728-1816), a General Baptist who sought, but ultimately failed, to bring renewal to his denomination in the latter part of the eighteenth century, put it: "They degraded Jesus Christ, and He degraded them."[2] Two other factors that arrested General Baptist growth were their distinct reluctance to erect church buildings and their strict enforcement of a policy of endogamy (confirming marriage to their own church family).

Then, it was the Calvinistic Baptists who recovered the view of baptism as a testimony to the death, burial, and resurrection of the Lord Jesus. The General Baptists regarded baptism primarily as an outward sign of the inner washing of the believer's heart. In other words, the Calvinistic Baptist view of baptism was substantially different from that of the General Baptists in the early years. Third, it was the Calvinistic Baptists in the early 1640s who rediscovered that baptism should be by immersion - the General Baptists had, up until that point in time, baptised by sprinkling or pouring. Finally, and this is most important, the Calvinistic Baptists have a somewhat different genesis than the General Baptists. Their reasons for embracing believer's baptism and the entire atmosphere out of which they emerged were considerably different from those of the General Baptists. One further point is that the Calvinistic Baptists reveal, in a much clearer fashion than the General Baptists, that Baptist origins are to be found in the Puritanism of the late sixteenth and early seventeenth centuries and not sixteenth-century continental Anabaptism. As such, these Baptists are the heirs of the sixteenth-century Reformed community and cannot be understood without reference to that movement.[3]

The Jacob-Lathrop-Jessey Church

Now, there is one church in particular which lies at the fountainhead of the Calvinistic Baptists and that is the London-based congregation known to historians as the Jacob-Lathrop-Jessey church, so-called because of the names of its first three pastors.[4] Henry Jacob (1563-1624) and a group of like-minded believers in London had established the congregation in 1616. To what extent Jacob and his congregation were influenced by Separatists like Francis Johnson and John Robinson remains an open question - Jacob met both of these men Johnson in 1599 and Robinson in 1610.[5] What is clear, however, is the fact that Jacob's congregation was determined not to cut itself off from all fellowship with Puritans who had stayed within the Church of England. In the statement of faith that this congregation published when it was first established, it was clearly stated that attendance at services conducted in local parish churches was permissible as long as "neither our assent, nor silent presence is given to any mere human tradition". Unlike the Separatists, Jacob and his congregation refused to deny that the Church of England still possessed "true visible churches", and thus it was not at all wrong to continue fellow shipping with them where this did not involve countenancing what Jacob's congregation regarded as definite error. It is not surprising that the authorities in the Church of England harassed the congregation as a Separatist body, and that the Separatists dubbed them "idolaters".[6]

Due to this harassment and persecution, Jacob decided to leave England for Virginia in 1622, where he died two years later. His successor was John Lathrop (1584-1653). During Lathrop's pastorate at least two groups amicably withdrew from the church to found Separatist congregations, one of which came to be pastored by a certain Samuel Eaton (d. 1639). Eaton had problems with the legitimacy of the baptism of infants by ministers in the Church of England, though it does not appear to be the case that he had actually come to embrace believer's baptism as the only basis for membership in the church.[7]

In the early 1630s, when William Laud (1573-1645), the Armenian Archbishop of Canterbury, was seeking to rid England of Puritanism, Lathrop also decided to emigrate to the New World. He left in 1634, and it was not until 1637 that a new pastor was found in the person of Henry Jessey (1601-1663).[8] Jessey had become a Puritan while studying at Cambridge in the early 1620s. Ordained a priest in the Church of England in 1626, he grew increasingly uneasy with the liturgy and worship of the Established Church over the next eight or so years. In 1635 he came into contact with the Jacob-Lathrop church, presumably began to worship with the congregation, and two years later was called to be the church's pastor. An ironic individual, Jessey continued to uphold the "Jacobite" tradition, that is, the policy established by Henry Jacob of keeping in fellowship with Puritans within the Church of England.

John Spilsbury and the first Calvinistic Baptist Church

A year or so after Jessey became the pastor of this church, the question of the validity of infant baptism arose. In a document drawn up at this time, the so-called *Kiffin Manuscript*, we read that in 1638 "Mr Tho: Wilson, Mr Pen & H. Pen, & 3 more being convinced that Baptism was not for Infants, but professed Believers [sic] joined with Mr Io: Spilsbury the Church's favour being desired therein".[9] John Spilsbury (1593-*ca.* 1668) was probably a cobbler by trade, and may have been a member of the Jacob-Lathrop-Jessey church at one point.[10] His church is clearly the first that can be definitely designated as a Calvinistic Baptist cause. For many years it met in an area of London called Wapping. By 1670 around three hundred regularly attended the services of the church. In later years it moved to Prescot Street, and then Commercial Street, and finally to Walthamstow, where from 1924 to 1934 it was pastored by Ernest Kevan. It still exists today and continues as a thriving evangelical work. Spilsbury wrote a number of small works that reveal his strong Calvinistic convictions. For example, in *God's Ordinance,*

The Saints' Privilege Spilsbury sounded forth one of the distinctive notes of the Calvinistic Baptist movement when he stated that "Christ hath not presented to his Father's justice a satisfaction for the sins of all men; but only for the sins of those that do or shall believe in him; which are his elect only."[11] It is vital to note that the Spilsbury congregation, which was probably little larger than a small house church when it began, maintained a good relationship with its mother church. There is evidence of joint gatherings for prayer and members of the Spilsbury congregation continued to attend meetings at the Jacob-Lathrop-Jessey church. Of all the various groups that eventually left this church, B. R. White has observed that "there were no high walls of bitterness between them and even the withdrawals are recorded as brotherly".[12]

By May of 1640 the Jacob-Lathrop-Jessey church had grown to the point that it was too large to meet in one place. The decision was thus taken to split the congregation into two, one half to continue under the pastoral leadership of Jessey and the other half under that of Praise-God Barebone (d. 1679). That same year Jessey's congregation was physically attacked by the Lord Mayor of London, Sir John Wright, who, according to one source, "came violently on them, beat, thrust, pinched, and kicked men or women as fled not his handling". Among those who were beaten was a pregnant woman named Mrs. Berry, who, as a result of her ill treatment, not only lost her baby in a miscarriage but also lost her own life.[13]

Richard Blunt and the mode of baptism

At roughly the same time as this external crisis, the question of baptism once again surfaced. An individual named Richard Blunt, who had left the Jacob-Lathrop-Jessey congregation in 1633 with Samuel Eaton, began to fellowship with the church once again in 1640. Blunt soon aired the question of whether or not the baptism of believers by immersion was the only type of baptism to actually correspond to that practised in New Testament times. It would appear that up until this point Spilsbury's congregation baptised believers by either sprinkling or pouring. According to the *Kiffin Manuscript*, "Mr Richard Blunt ... being convinced of Baptism yet also it ought to be by dipping ye Body into ye Water, resembling Burial & rising again. ...Col 2:12, Rom 6:4, had sober conference about in ye Church."[14] The texts that especially convinced Blunt that the baptism of believers should be by immersion are named here as Colossians 2:12 and Romans 6:4, both of which relate baptism to the believer's death, burial and resurrection with Christ. Blunt and those who were like-minded knew of no congregation in England who baptised believers by immersion and thus had no one close at hand to whom they could turn for instruction. Enquiries were made and it was discovered that there was a group of believers in the Netherlands who baptised by immersion, a Mennonite body known as the Collegiants. Blunt, who spoke Dutch, thus went to Holland to discuss the issue with them and presumably see a baptism at first-hand. The *Kiffin Manuscript* tells us that upon his return Blunt baptised a certain "Mr Blacklock who was a teacher amongst them, & Mr Blunt being Baptised, he & Mr Blacklock Baptised the rest of their friends that ware so minded", forty-one in all.[15] Two churches were formed: one pastored by Richard Blunt, the other by Thomas Kilcop. Among those baptised after Blunt's return from Holland was Mark Lucar (d. 1676), who played a significant role in the spread of Calvinistic Baptist principles in North America.[16] Soon after Blunt's return, Spilsbury and his congregation also adopted immersion as the proper mode of baptism. A fourth London Calvinistic Baptist congregation had also been planted by this time - in Crutched Fryers by John Green, a hat-maker, and John Spencer, a coachman.[17]

A debate about believer's baptism

Meanwhile Baptist principles had continued to spread in the Jacob-Lathrop-Jessey church. By 1644 Hanserd Knollys (*ca.* 1599-1691), who would become one of the key leaders of the Calvinistic Baptist cause during the seventeenth century and whose life will be treated more fully in chapter 6, had became convinced of believer's baptism and subsequently gave leadership to yet another group that withdrew from the Jacob-Lathrop-Jessey church to form a Calvinistic Baptist congregation. A good example of the defence of believer's baptism by these fledgling Baptist churches is found in *A Declaration concerning the Public Dispute ... concerning Infants Baptism*. This document, drawn up by Knollys together with two other leading Calvinistic Baptists, William Kiffin (1616-1701) and Benjamin Cox,[18] was published in 1645 after the cancellation of a public debate over the issue of baptism. The debate was cancelled when it was rumoured that these three Baptist leaders intended to bring "Swords, Clubs, and Staves" to enforce their point of view, and that the main spokesman for infant baptism, Edmund Calamy (1600-1666), a noted Presbyterian divine, would be fortunate to escape with his life![19]

Knollys, Kiffin and Cox forcefully argued that there is no text, either explicit or implied, in either the New or the Old Testaments in which there is to be a found a command to baptise infants.[20] Those who baptise infants, therefore, are adding to the commandments of Scripture and actually rob Christ of his honour as King and Lawgiver. Paedo-Baptists, the authors argued,

> undervalue the Kingly Office of Christ, in giving Laws to his Church in this; That they go about to perform (as they say) a duty to Christ, but can show no command for it from Christ; but must use their own Art and Reason to make Christ's Law strong enough to hold it out to be a duty. And whether the joining of man's Art, Policy, and Reason to the Laws of Christ doth not exceedingly undervalue Christ, as though his Laws were not perfect enough for his people, we leave the wise to judge. And in so doing, they do exceedingly take ... that Honour and Pre-eminency from him, which the Holy Spirit gives to him.[21]

The failure to abide by the commands of Scripture meant that those who defended infant baptism were actually guilty of engaging in "will-worship". This phrase, derived from Col. 2:23, was a frequent charge hurled by the Puritans against those in the Church of England who resisted their desired reforms. It castigated the worship so described as having its origin solely in the will and imagination of men and women. Behind the use of this phrase lay the Puritan conviction that all worship in the church must conform to what is explicitly commanded in Scripture. Puritans like Calamy, who did seek to order the worship of their churches according to this conviction, would have been particularly sensitive to, and nettled by, such a charge. But the Baptist leaders were simply logically applying this conviction to baptism. If all in the worship of the Church is to be done according to the Word, and there is no explicit command for the baptism of infants, then only that of believers is to be administered.

Knollys, Kiffin, and Cox also turned to such texts as Matthew 28:19, which they described as "the only written Commission to Baptise". This text directs the church to "baptize Disciples only". Due to the fact that infants as infants cannot learn about Christ and place their faith in him, they cannot be disciples, and thus should not be baptised.

Calamy was not convinced by such arguments, but other Puritans were, among them Henry Jessey. On June 29, 1645, Knollys had the joy of baptising his former pastor. Though Jessey had become personally convinced of believer's baptism, he refused to shed his irenicism. His congregation continued to accept into membership those who had been baptised as infants. Jessey's open membership policy thus set him apart from the Calvinistic Baptists, who insisted that every member of their local churches be a baptised believer. Jessey maintained friendly relations with the Calvinistic Baptists down till his death in 1663 - Knollys, in fact, was present when he died - but he was always a little fearful that they had gone too far in their closed membership principles and were actually idolising baptism.[22]   As far as the Calvinistic Baptists were concerned, however, they were simply seeking to be faithful to all of God's commands.

3.
The First London Confession of Faith

In mid-October, 1644, a bookseller by the name of George Thomason, who was located next to St. Paul's Churchyard in London, began to sell a small tract entitled "The Confession of Faith of those churches which are commonly (though falsely) called Anabaptists". The authors of this pamphlet were not named on the title-page, though at the foot of the introductory preface there did appear fifteen names - the pastoral leadership of the seven Calvinistic Baptist churches then in existence, all of them located in the capital. As to which of these leaders were the actual authors of this Confession, later known as the *First London Confession* of *Faith*, it appears that John Spilsbury, William Kiffin and Samuel Richardson played the most prominent role in drawing it up.[1]

The reasons for the Confession

They issued the Confession mainly to defend themselves against various false charges that were being circulated in the capital. As they explained in the preface they had been depicted as men and women "lying under that calumny and black brand of Heretics, and sowers of division". From the pulpits and in the writings of fellow Puritans, they had been accused of "holding Free-will, Falling away from grace, denying Originall sinne, disclaiming of Magistracy, denying to assist them either in persons or purse in any of their lawful Commands, doing acts unseemly in the dispensing the Ordinance of Baptism, not to be named amongst Christians".[2] From the first three of these charges it would appear that the Calvinistic Baptists were being confused with the General Baptists, who were explicitly Arminian in their theology. The next two charges are ones relating to political subversion and rebellion. Such accusations were probably levelled on the misunderstanding that the Calvinistic Baptists were akin to the revolutionary, continental Anabaptists of the previous century. It is noteworthy that in the title of their

Confession, the Calvinistic Baptists emphasised that they were "commonly (though falsely) called Anabaptists". The final charge - that of sexual immorality in the administration of baptism - was pure slander, but one that was frequently made against the early Baptists. For example, Daniel Featley (1582-1645), an influential, outspoken minister devoted to the Church of England and critical of Puritanism, penned a scurrilous attack on the Baptists entitled *The Dippers dipt. Or, The Anabaptists duck'd and plunged Over Head and Eares* (1645). In it he maintained that the Baptists were in the habit of stripping "stark naked, not onely when they flocke in great multitudes, men and women together, to their Jordans to be dipt; but also upon other occasions, when the season permits"![3]

The upshot of such charges - charges that the authors of this preface vehemently asserted were "notoriously untrue" - was that many godly believers wanted nothing at all to do with the Calvinistic Baptists and many unbelievers were encouraged, "if they can find the place of our meeting, to get together in Clusters to stone us, as looking upon us as a people ... not worthy to live".[4] John Spilsbury, for example, mentioned in 1643 that his convictions regarding believer's baptism had made his opponents "so incensed against me, as to seek my life".[5]

Consequently, in 1644 the London Calvinistic Baptist leadership decided to issue a confession of faith which would demonstrate once and for all their fundamental solidarity with the international Calvinist community. The *First London Confession of Faith* went through at least two printings that year, and on November 30, 1646 it was reissued in a second edition. This Confession seems to have accomplished its goal in defusing the criticism of many fellow Puritans and it soon became the doctrinal standard for the first period of Calvinistic Baptist advance, which ended in 1660 with the restoration of Charles II (r.1660-1685).[6]

The contents of the Confession

The 1644 edition of the Confession consists of fifty-three articles. The first twenty articles deal with the nature and attributes of God, the doctrine of the Trinity, divine election, the fall and sinfulness of all humanity, and the person and work of Christ in his offices of prophet, priest, and king. Articles XXI to XXXII deal with the work of salvation and unequivocally reveal the Confession's Calvinism.[7]

For instance, Article XXII, discussing saving faith, states that "Faith is the gift of God wrought in the hearts of the elect by the Spirit of God."[8] And as the gift of God, this faith cannot be lost, as Article XXIII declares: "Those that have this precious faith wrought in them by the Spirit, can never finally nor totally fall away."[9] Moreover, such saving faith is possessed only by the elect of God. In the words of Article XXI: "Christ Jesus by his death did bring forth salvation and reconciliation only for the elect, which were those which God the Father gave him."[10] Yet, as Robert W. Oliver has noted, this "belief in Particular Redemption did not inhibit evangelism". In the same article which committed those who signed this Confession to particular redemption, we also read that "the Gospel ... is to be preached to all men".[11]

The final five articles of the Confession effectively rebut the charge that the London Calvinistic Baptists were Anabaptist revolutionaries by emphasising that the civil power is ordained by God and that this power is not only to be obeyed, but also defended in all civil matters.[12] In the second edition of 1646 a further article was added which stated that it was perfectly legitimate for "a Christian to be a Magistrate or Civill Officer" and "to take an Oath", both of which the continental Anabaptists of the sixteenth century had disputed.[13]

The ecclesiology of the Confession

The fifteen articles that lie between those discussing God's work in the salvation of sinners and those detailing the relationship of local churches to the state contain a thorough discussion of the nature of the church and its life. The local church, Article XXXIII affirms, "is a company of visible Saints, called & separated from the world, by the word and the Spirit of God, to the visible profession of the faith of the Gospel, being baptised into that faith, and joined to the Lord, and each other, by mutual agreement".[14] In other words, the local church should consist only of those who have professed faith in Christ and have borne visible witness to that faith by being baptised. What is meant by placing baptism after the profession of faith in this article is later made explicit in Articles XXXIX and XL.[15] In the first of these articles, it is clearly stated that only those who have professed faith or who are "Disciples, or taught upon a profession of faith, ought to be baptised".[16]

Article XL then goes on to describe the proper mode and meaning of baptism. It should be by immersion, or by "dipping or plunging the whole body under water". As to its meaning, the authors of the Confession noted three significations of baptism. First, it bears witness to the inner washing of the believer by the blood of Christ. In later editions of the Confession this meaning was omitted. Second, it signifies the believer's "death, burial, and resurrection" with Christ. Finally, it helps to give the believer assurance that, just as he or she is raised up from the waters of baptism, "so certainly shall the bodies of the Saints be raised by the power of Christ, in the day of the resurrection". In the margin alongside this article there was also a pointed refutation of the charge that the Baptists, in their administration of the ordinance of baptism, engaged in acts of immorality. The baptism of believers was carried out, it said, with "convenient garments both upon the administrator and subject, with all modesty".[17]

In entering the local church through the doorway of baptism, believers are declaring their acknowledgement of Christ as "their Prophet, Priest, and King" and placing themselves under "his heavenly conduct and government, to lead their lives in his walled sheep-fold, and watered garden" (Article XXXIV).[18] The final image used here to describe the church, "watered garden", would have a noteworthy history among the Calvinistic Baptists. The phrase is drawn from the Song of Solomon 4:12: "A garden inclosed is my sister, my spouse; a spring shut up, a fountain sealed" (KJV) and over the next century it would recur again and again in Calvinistic Baptist documents that talked about the nature of the church.[19]

A significant number of homes in seventeenth-century England had enclosed gardens attached to them. While some of these gardens were developed for aesthetic reasons and consisted primarily of flowers and shrubs, many of them were kitchen gardens, designed to produce small fruits, herbs, salad greens and other vegetables. Generally rectangular in shape, they were enclosed by walls, fences or hedges that might reach as high as sixteen feet. These walls provided both protection from the cooling effects of the wind and privacy for the owner.[20] In fact, during the turbulent era of the 1640s, when the British Isles experienced the horrors and ravage of civil war, such gardens came to be increasingly seen as "places of secure retreat from the dangers of political and religious strife".[21]

Given the insularity of such enclosed gardens, the increased use of this term by Calvinistic Baptists in the late seventeenth and the early eighteenth centuries as a favoured description of their churches can hardly be considered fortuitous. For as the Calvinistic Baptists moved into the eighteenth century their community was increasingly insular. The use of this phrase, with all of its introspective overtones, would only help to encourage further the Calvinistic Baptists to closet themselves within their meeting houses and limit their horizons to the maintenance of church life. But all of this was far in the future when this Confession was drafted, and the men who drew it up were far from being inward-looking. As we have noted, they were firmly convinced that "the Gospel ... is to be preached to all men".

Article XXXV went on to note that every believer in the local church has been gifted for service. "All his [i.e. Christ's] servants are called thither [i.e. to the church], to present their bodies and souls, and to bring their gifts God hath given them; so being come, they are here by himself bestowed in their several order, peculiar place, due use, being fitly compact and knit together, according to the effectual working of every part, to the edification of itself in love."[22] The Confession assumes that God has endowed every believer with at least one spiritual gift and, as true servants of Christ, believers are "to bring their gifts" to the church, where they can be employed in edifying and building up the body of Christ. A later article, Article XLV, explicitly identifies one of these gifts. "Such to whom God hath given gifts," this article stated, "being tryed in the Church, may and ought by the appointment of the Congregation, to prophesie, according to the proportion of faith, and so teach publicly the Word of God, for the edification, exhortation and comfort of the Church."[23]

Now, in General Baptist circles it was believed that the New Testament gift of prophecy was being exercised when, as regularly happened, members of the congregation rose and delivered extemporaneous messages after, or even in place of, the sermon.[24] This practice, though, does not seem to be what is in view in the text cited above from the *First London Confession*. Those who "prophesie" have been recognised by the congregation as being especially gifted in the public teaching of God's Word, and by the "appointment of the Congregation" exercise a regular ministry in this regard. A similar interpretation of the gift of prophecy can be

found in a work by Hanserd Knollys, who would sign the second
edition of the Confession in 1646. In *An Exposition of the Whole
Book of the Revelation,* he makes the following comment on
Revelation 11:3, which talks about the prophetic ministry of the two
witnesses: "[The] Gift of Prophecy Christ gives unto his faithful
Ministers in the Churches of Saints, that they may be his Witnesses
... in bearing their Testimony for Christ ... in all the Offices of his
Mediatorship."[25]

Articles XXXVI, XLII to XLV are a classic description of
congregational church government. On the basis of Matthew 18:17
and 1 Corinthians 5:4, it is affirmed that "Christ has ... given power
to his whole Church to receive in and cast out, by way of
Excommunication, any member; and this power is given to every
particular Congregation, and not one particular person, either
member or Officer, but the whole."[26] The members of the local
church acting together have the authority and power to receive new
members into their midst as well as to excommunicate those who
refuse to walk under Christ's lordship. Furthermore, "every church
has power given them from Christ, to choose to themselves meet
persons into the office of Pastors, Teachers, Elders, Deacons"
(Article XXXVI).[27] It was also stressed that "none other have power
to impose" leaders on the congregation from the outside. While later
editions will limit the names of the leaders of the congregation to
"Elders" and "Deacons", there will be no retreat from the fact that
"the ministry was ... firmly subordinated to the immediate authority
of the covenanted community".[28] As B. R. White has pointed out,
this jealous concern for congregational autonomy was motivated by
a deep desire to be free to obey Christ, and not to be bound by the
dictates of men and human traditions.[29] In sum, Christ has entrusted
to individual congregations the authority and right to order their
lives together as believers. The understanding of the local church
displayed in these articles places upon church members a great
responsibility. In the words of Stanley Grenz, professor of theology
at Carey Hall in Vancouver:

> Believers are initiated into a corporate life in which they are
> to become personally involved and over which they are to
> take personal ownership. Because the people are the church,
> ongoing Baptist congregational life demands the involve-
> ment of each member in a way unparalleled by the leader-
> centred polity of both the traditional churches and the newer
> charismatic groups.[30]

Early Baptist Associations

This strong affirmation of congregational autonomy in the texts cited above, which could easily lead to isolationism, was balanced by Article XLVII, in which it was stated that "although the particular Congregations be distinct and several Bodies, every one a compact and knit Citie in itselfe; yet are they all to walk by one and the same Rule, and by all means convenient to have the counsel and help of one another in all needful affairs of the Church, as members of one body in the common faith under Christ their only head."[31] The autonomy of each local congregation is recognised as a biblical given, but so is the fact that each congregation ultimately belongs to only one Body and each shares the same head, the Lord Christ. Therefore, local congregations should endeavour to help one another.

The sort of help envisioned by the authors of this Confession can be discerned in the proof texts that were placed alongside this article in both its 1644 and 1646 editions. The first edition cited, among other verses, 1 Corinthians 16:1, which refers to the collection of money that Paul gathered from congregations in Greece and Asia Minor for the poor in the church at Jerusalem, and Colossians 4:16, in which the church at Colossae is urged to share Paul's letter to them with the church at Laodicea and vice versa. In the 1646 edition, some proof texts were dropped and among those added were Acts 15:2-3, which deals with the Jerusalem Council, and 2 Corinthians 8:1,4, which also has to do with the collection of money for the church at Jerusalem. In other words, the authors of this Confession envisioned the churches helping one another in areas of financial need as well as in giving advice with regard to doctrinal and ethical matters. Ultimately what bound the churches together was a common determination to walk according to the "one and the same Rule", that is, the Scriptures. Only where there is such genuine agreement as to the source of final authority for life and doctrine can local churches walk and work together.[32]

Here, in Article XLVII, is the genesis of what would later become a characteristic feature of the early Calvinistic Baptists, namely, their regional Associations which linked together local congregations in specific geographical areas of Great Britain. And if it is asked from whence the signatories of the Confession derived their convictions in this regard, the experience that many of them had had in the Jacob-Lathrop-Jessey congregation immediately comes to mind. There, they had experienced a church life that was far from being isolationist and that had consciously striven to nurture bonds between itself and other congregations.[33]

These associations were to be a key factor in the great growth that the Calvinistic Baptist cause witnessed during the late 1640s and the 1650s. These were tumultuous years in English history, as the land was convulsed in civil war and experienced massive social, political, and economic upheaval. The Calvinistic Baptists flourished, however, and their commitment to Associations played a vital part in their growth. Associations provided mutual strength and fellowship, an instrument for preserving congregational integrity and orthodoxy, a means of providing for the financial needs of poorer congregations, and a way of supporting church-planting and evangelistic endeavours. The important place that these first-generation Baptists accorded to their Associations is well expressed by White when he states that "they no more believed that an individual congregation should be free to go its own way than that an individual believer could be a serious Christian without commitment to a local, visible congregation".[34]

The Calvinistic Baptist cause expanded from the seven churches in London in the mid-1640s to around 130 throughout England, Wales and Ireland by the late 1650s. It was indeed a unique time of spiritual harvest and blessing. And helping to win converts to the Baptist position and bind them together was the *First London Confession of Faith*.

William Kiffin (1616-1701)

4.
William Kiffin (1616-1701), "A Lover of Peace and Truth"

When Joseph Ivimey (1773-1834), the nineteenth-century Baptist historian, published the life of William Kiffin in 1833 he did so in the conviction that Kiffin was "one of the most extraordinary persons whom the [Calvinistic Baptist] denomination has produced, both as to the consistency and correctness of his principles and the eminence of his worldly and religious character". Ivimey especially hoped that this account of Kiffin's life and ministry would spur his younger Baptist contemporaries to take Kiffin as "a pattern of piety and integrity".[1] To what degree this hope was realized cannot be pursued here; but, in the more than a century and a half between Ivimey's day and the present, Kiffin's remarkable life has been increasingly known solely to scholars studying the origins and rise of the Calvinistic Baptists in seventeenth-century England.

In an article written nearly twenty-five years ago, Barrie R. White stated that there was still no adequate biography of Kiffin.[2] The intervening quarter of a century has seen no real alteration in this situation. This fact is to be lamented, for Kiffin had, in White's words, "a unique place of honour and influence" amongst the early English Calvinistic Baptists. For instance, of those who signed the *First London Confession of Faith* in 1644, only Kiffin remained alive in 1689 to invite representatives of Calvinistic Baptist churches throughout England and Wales to gather in London for their first national assembly. It was at this assembly that these representatives approved the *Second London Confession of Faith*, a confession that has been well described as "the most influential and important of all Baptist Confessions".[3] And the second name on the list of those who gave their formal approval to this Confession was that of Kiffin, who signed for the church that he pastored at Devonshire Square in London. From the 1640s till his death at the beginning of the next century Kiffin was a source of strength and stability to the Calvinistic Baptist movement, and played a vital role in its growth and advance.

Conversion and early Christian experience

Born in London in 1616, Kiffin was orphaned at the young age of nine, when his parents died of an outbreak of the plague. In 1629, Kiffin was apprenticed to a glover,[4] but two years later, in his own words, "growing melancholy", he decided to run away from his master.[5] Providentially he happened to go by St. Antholin's Church, where the Puritan Thomas Foxley (fl. 1640) was preaching that day on "the duty of servants to masters". Seeing a crowd of people going into the church, Kiffin decided to join them. As has been the experience of many under the Spirit-anointed preaching of the Word, Kiffin was convinced that Foxley's sermon was intentionally directed at him. He returned home to his master with the resolve "to hear some more of them, whom they called Puritan ministers".[6] After regularly listening to a number of Puritan preachers, including John Davenport (1597-1670) and Lewis Du Moulin (1606-1680), it was the preaching of the Arminian John Goodwin (*ca.* 1594-1665) which God eventually used to bring Kiffin to Christ.

Shortly after his conversion Kiffin became a member of a group of zealous young men, who made it their habit to attend an early morning preaching service. Prior to the service, which began at six in the morning, Kiffin and his friends would, in Kiffin's words:

> Meet together an hour before service, to spend it in prayer, and in communicating to each other what experience we had received from the Lord; or else to repeat some sermon which we had heard before. After a little time, we also read some portion of Scripture, and spake from it what it pleased God to enable us; wherein I found very great advantage, and by degrees did arrive at some small measure of knowledge. I found the study of the Scriptures very pleasant and delightful to me.[7]

As White has pointed out, this passage admirably displays the way in which Kiffin was prepared theologically and spiritually to lead a Calvinistic Baptist congregation for nearly sixty years. Like most of the early Calvinistic Baptist leaders, Kiffin did not have a formal theological education.[8] He became skilled in the knowledge and use of the Scriptures as he first regularly listened to the preaching of the Word, then shared with others its impact on his life, and finally preached on various Scriptures as the Lord enabled him.

During the 1630s Puritans within the Church of England, like Kiffin, came under extreme pressure to bring their thinking and behaviour into line with the views of William Laud, who became Archbishop of Canterbury in 1633. Laud was strongly Arminian in his theology, as well as being firmly convinced that the ritual of the Church of England, such as the wearing of vestments by ministers, the ornamentation of the communion table, and the use of the sign of the cross in the baptismal service, had the full approval of God. He sought to impose uniformity of ritual and doctrine in the Church of England, and refused to make any allowance for the individual conscience. Rather than conform, a goodly number of individuals left England either for the Netherlands or for New England. Others, though, refused to quit their homeland and formed or joined what the Church of England regarded as illegal congregations. Amongst the latter group was Kiffin.

Baptist convictions

When Kiffin wrote *A Sober Discourse of Right to Church-Communion* many years later, he mentioned that during this period in the late 1630s and early 1640s he had diligently searched the Scriptures "with earnest desires of God, that I might be directed in a right way of worship".[9] This searching of the Scriptures led him to quit the state church in 1638 and join himself to the independent congregation which had at one time been led by Samuel Eaton. When Kiffin joined this congregation, though, Eaton was in prison, where he would die the following year, and the church was pastorless. Kiffin was invited to preach to the congregation, and at some point over the course of the next three or four years he was chosen as their pastor. During this period Kiffin continued to study God's Word for direction with regard to the constitution and form of the church. By the fall of 1642 he, and the congregation, had arrived at a decidedly Baptist position.[10] As he wrote in his *Sober Discourse*, he came to the conviction that the "safest way" for him to follow in his Christian life was to step in "the Footsteps of the Flock (namely) that order laid down by Christ and His Apostles, and Practised by the Primitive Christians in their times which I found to be that after Conversion they were Baptised, added to the Church, and Continued in the Apostles' Doctrine, Fellowship, Breaking of Bread, and Prayer; according to which I thought myself bound to be

Conformable".[11] This text and the one cited above regarding Kiffin's early spiritual development well illustrate what B. A. Ramsbottom, an English author who has written widely on figures in Calvinistic Baptist history, has argued is the key to Kiffin's life, namely, his earnest desire to follow the Scriptures whatever the cost.[12]

As we have noted, by 1644 there were seven Calvinistic Baptist congregations in England, including the one pastored by Kiffin. In that year, as we have discussed above in Chapter 3, these churches issued the *First London Confession of Faith*, in the drafting of which Kiffin appears to have played a significant role. Given Kiffin's later closed communion position, it is noteworthy that the 1644 edition of this Confession has no explicit statement regarding the relationship between baptism and the Lord's Supper. The second edition, however, did specify that only those who were baptised should partake of the Lord's Table.[13]

Support for Oliver Cromwell

The late 1640s and early 1650s saw this Confession reprinted a number of times, clear evidence of the growth of the Calvinistic Baptist cause. Kiffin played a prominent role in this growth, planning the establishment of new churches and associations, giving them advice and counsel, and generally providing stability to the fledgling cause.[14] It was a tumultuous period when the steadying hand of men like Kiffin was greatly needed, for this was the time of the English Civil Wars, during which the king, Charles I (r. 1625-1649), was executed and a republican government set up.

The ensuing period, between the execution of Charles and the restoration of the monarchy in 1660, has become known as the Commonwealth. Heading the government for most of this period was Oliver Cromwell (1599-1658), of whom John Maidstone, Cromwell's valet, once remarked: "A larger soul hath seldom dwelt in a house of clay."[15] One of the most tolerant men of the seventeenth century, Cromwell viewed the English Civil Wars as principally a war for religious freedom. He longed to create an England where liberty of conscience was recognised as a "fundamental" and "natural right".[16] He had seen men and women forced by Archbishop Laud to leave England for the "vast howling wilderness in New England" in order to enjoy religious liberty, and, as a result, he was determined that such religious persecution would never occur again. According to the one-time Baptist Roger Williams (1603-1683), Cromwell once maintained in a public discussion "with much Christian zeal and affection... that he had rather that Mahumetanism [i.e. Mohammedanism] were permitted amongst us, than that one of God's children should be persecuted".[17]

Kiffin and many of his fellow Calvinistic Baptists were strong supporters of the Cromwellian government and this out of loyalty to what they saw as the God-ordained authorities, satisfaction with Cromwell's policy of toleration, and a deep-seated fear of anarchy. In fact, Kiffin sat as a member of Parliament for Middlesex in 1656. However, there were a number of Calvinistic Baptists, especially some in the army in Ireland, who were highly vocal in their criticism of Cromwell. Kiffin, John Spilsbury, and a Joseph Sansom wrote to their Irish Baptist brethren in January 1654, urging them to "consult with that blessed rule of truth which you profess to be your guide, ... for that expresseth no other thing to Christians but exhortations to be subject to all civil powers, they being of God, and to pray for all that are in authority, that under them we may live a godly and quiet life in all godliness and honesty". This letter by Kiffin and Spilsbury was especially critical of what has been termed the Fifth Monarchy movement, a group of individuals who believed that the prophecies of Daniel 2 were going to be literally fulfilled in their lifetime and that Christ's millenarian kingdom was shortly to be established. While one wing of the Fifth Monarchy movement was moderate, non-violent and included men like Henry Jessey - "harmless Bible students" - others had definite revolutionary tendencies and were convinced that they should take an active, even violent, role in the fulfilment of the prophecies of Daniel 2. Seeking to counteract the influence of the Fifth Monarchists on the Irish Baptists, Kiffin, Spilsbury, and Sansom urged the latter to reflect upon the fact that the Calvinistic Baptists in the British Isles had a marvellous opportunity to "give a public testimony in the face of the world, that our principles are not such as they have been generally judged by most men to be, which is, we deny authority, and would pull down all magistracy."[18]

An especially critical moment came in May of 1658, when, at the meeting of the Western Association of Baptist churches in Dorchester, some individuals who were sympathetic to the potentially subversive politics of the Fifth Monarchists sought to convince the representatives of the churches in the Association to publicly espouse the ideals and goals of the Fifth Monarchy party. Kiffin, who was present with other representatives from the churches in London, successfully persuaded the Western Association not to commit itself in this direction.[19] As Kiffin's letter to the Irish Baptists had noted, open and widespread adherence to these views by the Calvinistic Baptists would have had harmful and serious repercussions for their movement as a whole.

Also during these years Kiffin was extensively engaged as a merchant in the cloth trade. So successful were his trading ventures that he soon attained to great wealth. Despite this rapid ascent from poverty to riches, Kiffin, as White notes, "seems to have remained unspoiled".[20] Moreover, "the wealth which he acquired in the world of commerce conferred upon him a position which, during the dark and hectic days of persecution, he was able to use for the protection and defence of his poorer brethren."[21] These days of persecution began with the restoration of the monarchy in the person of Charles II (r. 1660-1685), the eldest surviving son of Charles I, who had been living in exile on the continent since 1651.

Kiffin and the House of Stuart

After the death of Oliver Cromwell in 1658 and when no leader of like calibre emerged, it seemed to some of the key figures in the army that England was slipping into anarchy. The decision was therefore made to invite Charles II back to England to assume the throne. Charles had promised religious toleration prior to his restoration, but almost immediately after his assumption of power independent congregations began to experience the fire of persecution, and for much of the next three decades the church would be "the church under the cross". Kiffin was jailed a number of times in the two or three years following Charles' restoration, but only for quite short periods of time. The blessings of liberty and influence which God had given to Kiffin were not lost on him. On a number of occasions he used his position and wealth to intervene on behalf of fellow Dissenters. For instance, in 1664 he was able to rescue twelve General Baptists, who had been sentenced to death for participating in an illegal conventicle. When Kiffin was informed of the plight of these individuals, he went directly to the king and obtained from him a reprieve for all of them.[22]

In fact, Kiffin appears to have been on quite good terms with the king. According to a story which has come down to us from Thomas Crosby, the eighteenth-century Baptist historian, Charles was once in need of a large sum of money. He asked Kiffin for a loan of forty thousand pounds! Kiffin, it seems, was aware that if he gave the king such a loan there was every likelihood that it would never be repaid. He thus offered to make the king a gift of ten thousand pounds, which the king gladly accepted. Afterwards, when he recounted the story, Kiffin jocosely remarked that he had thereby saved thirty thousand pounds![23]

Nevertheless, Kiffin's great wealth was of little avail during what was a deeply distressing event for him in the final years of this period of persecution. Upon the death of Charles II in 1685, his brother, the Roman Catholic James II (r. 1685-1688), succeeded to the throne. A good number of people, though, regarded the Duke of Monmouth, a professing Protestant and an illegitimate son of Charles II, as the rightful heir. A rebellion was fomented in the Duke's favour during the summer of 1685, but it was eventually crushed by James with much bloodshed. Among those who had supported the Duke's bid for power were two of Kiffin's grandsons, William and Benjamin Hewling. Both were apprehended after the failure of the rebellion, tried and executed. Kiffin unsuccessfully sought to obtain their freedom by offering three thousand pounds for their acquittal. In his words: "We missed the right door, for the lord chief justice [Jefferies] finding that agreements were made with others, and so little attention paid to himself, was the more provoked to use all manner of cruelty to the poor prisoners; so that few escaped."[24] Jefferies, who sentenced the Hewlings to death, actually told William Hewling during his trial that "his grandfather did as well deserve the death which he was likely to suffer, as himself".[25]

Within three years, however, Jefferies was himself imprisoned and James II an exile on the continent, as James' régime crumbled before the Glorious Revolution of 1688. This revolution, which put William of Orange on the throne as William III,[26] meant the dawn of a new era for Dissenters like Kiffin. In 1689 William III authorised the passing of the Act of Toleration, which gave Dissenters both freedom of worship and immunity from persecution, although certain civil restrictions against them remained in force.

Kiffin and the issue of closed communion

Kiffin, along with other Baptist leaders in London, took the opportunity that this turn of events afforded to issue a call in July of 1689 for a national assembly of Calvinistic Baptists, the first ever of its kind. Representatives from over one hundred churches gathered. Amongst other things, they gave thanks to God for "raising up our present King William, to be a blessed Instrument, in his Hand, to deliver us from Popery and Arbitrary Power".[27] And they approved the adoption of a confession of faith known as the *Second London Confession of Faith*, which had been drawn up originally in 1677 by William Collins (d. 1702) and Nehemiah Coxe (d. 1689), co-pastors of the Petty France Church in London. This Confession will be discussed in more detail in Chapter 6.

One point that should be noted here is the fact that closed communion, a requirement in the second edition of the *First London Confession*, is absent from the *Second London Confession*. In an appendix attached to the Confession when it was first issued in 1677, it was stated:

> We are not insensible that as to the order of God's house, and entire communion therein there are some things wherein we (as well as others) are not at a full accord among our selves, as for instance; the known principle, and state of the consciences of diverse of us, that have agreed in this Confession is such; that we cannot hold Church-communion, with any other than Baptised believers, and Churches constituted of such; yet some others of us have a greater liberty and freedom in our spirits that way; and therefore we have purposely omitted the mention of things of that nature, that we might concur, in giving this evidence of our agreement, both among our selves, and with other good Christians, in those important articles of the Christian Religion, mainly insisted on by us.[28]

One of the reasons for this difference between the two confessions is that Nehemiah Coxe, who was intimately involved in drawing up the *Second London Confession*, had been called to the ministry in 1672 by the open communion, open membership church in Bedford which John Bunyan (1628-1688) pastored from 1672 till his death sixteen years later.[29] Moreover, Petty France Church in London, which Coxe later pastored, regularly received into its membership believers from open communion Calvinistic Baptist churches.[30] Even more significant was the fact that by 1677, both open and closed communion Calvinistic Baptist churches had experienced seventeen years of persecution. In Robert W. Oliver's words, "Disunity was a luxury that they could ill afford."[31]

The assembly at which the *Second London Confession* was adopted also passed a resolution to the effect that the churches were to be given the liberty to follow their own judgment when it came to open or closed communion. This resolution read as follows: "In those things wherein one church differs from another church in their principles or practices, in point of communion, ... we cannot, shall not impose upon any particular church therein, but leave every church to their own liberty to walk together as they have received from the Lord."[32] A. C. Underwood and Joshua Thompson, both twentieth-century Baptist historians, have understood this resolution to mean that while fellowship and recognition was to be extended to open communion churches with closed membership, it was not to be extended to those churches which, like Bunyan's, held to both open communion and open membership.[33] Yet, as White has pointed out, there was at least one open membership church which sent a representative to this Calvinistic Baptist Assembly in 1689, namely, Broadmead Church in Bristol.[34] Believer's baptism and a personal profession of faith before the church were the normal requirements for admission to membership in this church, but on occasion some were received into membership solely on the basis of a personal testimony.[35]

Now, what is significant about these statements regarding open and closed communion is the fact that in the 1670s and the early 1680s, Kiffin had been involved in a lengthy controversy with none other than John Bunyan over this very issue. In fact, this controversy drew forth from Kiffin his most important work, *A Sober Discourse of Right to Church-Communion* (1681), a studied and heartfelt response to a series of treatises by John Bunyan in favour of open communion and open membership. Although Bunyan is currently one of the most celebrated Christian authors of the seventeenth century, in his own day he had little influence amongst his fellow Baptists.[36] His strong commitment to open communion and open membership put him out of step with most seventeenth-century

Calvinistic Baptists, who favoured closed communion and closed membership. Kiffin's *Sober Discourse* is characterised by "clear logic and crisp presentation", and is undoubtedly aimed at Bunyan, although the Bedford pastor is never explicitly named in the work. From Kiffin's perspective, the practice of open communion and open membership "destroys Order and flatly contradicts the Practice of the Primitive Christians". The "right Gospel Order" is laid down in Acts 2:41-42, where believers are first baptised, then "received into Church-fellowship", and only then share in the Lord's Table.[37] Yet the fact that eight years after Kiffin had published this defence of closed communion and closed membership he signed the *Second London Confession* indicates that by 1689 the London Baptist leader was clearly willing to agree to differ on the issue.

Final years

During Kiffin's final years he continued to be active in his pastorate at Devonshire Square and in the life of the English Calvinistic Baptists as a whole. For instance, it was to Kiffin that two Calvinistic Baptist churches looked for help on separate occasions when they were at odds among themselves. As White remarks, "Perhaps there can be no higher testimony of their esteem!"[38]

However, these were also years of domestic tragedy for Kiffin. Three of his children, as well as his first wife Hanna, had already died by this time: William, his eldest, at the age of twenty in 1669; a second son in Venice who, Kiffin asserted, was poisoned by a Roman Catholic priest;[39] a daughter, Priscilla, in 1679; Hanna in 1682. Respecting his wife's life and death, Kiffin wrote later:

> It pleased the Lord to take to himself, my dear and faithful wife, with whom I had lived nearly forty-four years; whose tenderness to me, and faithfulness to God, were such as cannot, by me, be expressed, as she constantly sympathised with me in all my afflictions. I can truly say, I never heard her utter the least discontent under all the various providences that attended either me or her; she eyed the hand of God in all our sorrows, so as constantly to encourage me in the ways of God: her death was the greatest sorrow to me that ever I met with in the world.[40]

Kiffin's second wife, Sarah, however, was cut of a different cloth. On March 2, 1698, she was charged with a number of misdeeds by Devonshire Square Church. Upon examination, she was found guilty of, among other things, defrauding her husband of two hundred pounds and making false accusations about him. When she refused to appear before the congregation, Sarah was suspended from communion on April 24, 1698.[41] To add sorrow upon sorrow, a third son, Harry, passed away on December 8, 1698. Without a doubt, these events must have caused Kiffin deep anguish; but he did not waver in his commitment to the One whom he had served for most of his life. As he had written in 1693 at the conclusion of his memoirs: "The world is full of confusions: the last times are upon us: the signs of the times are very visible: iniquity abounds, and the love of many in religion waxes cold. God is, by his providence, shaking the earth under our feet; there is no sure foundation of rest and peace, but only in Jesus Christ."[42]

He fell asleep in Christ on December 29, 1701 and was buried in Bunhill Fields, his life indeed having been that of "a Lover of Truth and Peace", the self-description that he had placed on the title-page of *A Sober Discourse of Right to Church-Communion.*

Hanserd Knollys (1599-1691)

5.
Hanserd Knollys (ca. 1599-1691), "That Old Disciple of Jesus Christ"

Hanserd Knollys was the only significant Calvinistic Baptist leader, apart from William Kiffin, who experienced the golden days of the 1640s and 1650s and who lived to see the toleration extended by William III to them and other Nonconformists in 1688 after they had been persecuted for close to three decades.[1] Unlike Kiffin and most of his fellow Baptists, Knollys had received a university education. He had studied at St. Catherine Hall in Cambridge University where, in his words, "I prayed daily, heard all the godly ministers I could, read and searched the holy scriptures, read good books, got acquainted with gracious Christians then called Puritans".[2] After going down from Cambridge, Knollys was ordained and appointed minister of the parish church at Humberstone in Lincolnshire.[3] Knollys, however, eventually felt constrained to resign this charge in 1631 because, among other things, he could no longer use the sign of the cross in baptism or continue "admitting wicked persons to the Lord's Supper".[4]

By 1635 Knollys had made a complete break with the Church of England, and left England for America. However, he ran into trouble with the New England Congregationalists and decided to return to England in the autumn of 1641. Within three years he had come to hold to believer's baptism and to identify himself with the fledgling Calvinistic Baptist cause centred on London. Knollys' identification with the Calvinistic Baptists led initially to a controversial preaching tour in Suffolk, during which, on one occasion, a "rude multitude" prevented him from preaching by casting stones at him while he was in the pulpit.[5] It was also during this preaching tour that he gave the sermon which he later published as *Christ Exalted*, an excellent example of the Christ-centred spirituality of the early Calvinistic Baptists and which we will look at in more detail shortly. This preaching tour was followed by a couple of publications defending Baptist beliefs, his involvement as a champion of the Baptist cause in a number of formal debates, and his signing the second edition of the *First London Confession*, published in 1646.

Knollys signed this Confession as the pastor of a substantial London congregation, which may well have regularly seen close to a thousand come to hear him preach in the late 1640s and 1650s.[6] Throughout these years, however, Knollys was active not only in promoting the Baptist cause in London, but also in seeking to establish Baptist works in other areas of England and Wales. As has already been mentioned, these years were a harvest-time for the Calvinistic Baptists. Taking advantage of the religious toleration extended to them by Oliver Cromwell they were able to plant some 130 churches in these two decades,[7] and Knollys played a key role in this expansion.

Knollys and the Seekers

Now, in championing the Baptist cause Knollys had to deal with the attacks of an amorphous group known as the Seekers, who flourished during the 1640s and the 1650s. The Seekers, J. F. McGregor points out, regarded the sign of a true church of Christ to be "its possession of the grace given to the apostles and demonstrated through miracles". Thus, since none of the Puritan congregations claimed to be in possession of such charismatic gifts, the Seekers felt that they had to withdraw from them and wait for what they hoped would be a new divine dispensation.[8]

William Erbery (1604-1654),[9] for instance, who began his career as a Puritan vicar in Cardiff and ended up as "the champion of the Seekers", argued that he and his contemporaries were living in an era characterised by the absence of the life-giving Spirit of God. The Spirit had withdrawn from the church after the days of the apostles because of the church's apostate ways. Due to this absence of the Spirit and his charismatic gifts, any attempt to gather churches on the basis of what the New Testament has to say about the local church and its ordinances was doomed to failure. On the basis of this perspective Erbery judged the Calvinistic Baptists to be sorely deluded in their attempt to establish New Testament congregations. The apostles, he asserted, could baptise believers because they "had the manifestation of the Spirit in manifold gifts", but, he asked, "what manifestation of the Spirit have any of the Churches this day?"[10] In fact, Erbery maintained, Old Testament believers were in a better state than believers in his day: "The Church, under the Law, had some gifts of the Spirit manifest among them, as the gift of Prophecy, the gift of Healing, yea raising the Dead, with signs and miracles ...; this is more than present Churches have, having less of the manifestation of the Spirit than that under the Law, therefore [they] must needs be more in bondage in Babylon, not having one gift of the Spirit to continue their Church-state to be of a Gospel-glory".[11] Thus, because the Baptist congregations

> have not the appearance of the Spirit from on high, the Lord will roar in them, and will make every one of them to tremble ... because therein they disobey the command of Christ; they tell their proselytes, You must be dipt, because you must obey the command of Christ, I say, going forth to baptise, or be baptised, without the baptism of the Spirit on the Church, is not the command of Christ, but against it. ... What is the baptism of the Spirit? Is it the presence of the Spirit? The apostles had the presence of the Spirit before [Pentecost]; Is it the abundance of the Spirit? Christ breathed upon them before [Pentecost], and said, "Receive the holy Spirit," John 20:22, yet they were not baptized with the Spirit. The baptism of the Spirit (as I have often said) is pouring forth of all the gifts of the Spirit on the Church. ... Therefore to Baptise in a Gospel-way without the Baptism of the Spirit, is to deny the Spirit of Jesus.[12]

Illustrative of the Calvinistic Baptist answer to the Seeker position is Knollys' *The Shining of a Flaming Fire in Zion*, published in 1646. This book was a reply to a pamphlet written by the radical Puritan John Saltmarsh (*ca.* 1612-1647), which was entitled *The Smoke in the Temple* (1646).[13] In this pamphlet, Saltmarsh, though not a Seeker himself, accurately summarised a number of the Seeker arguments against the Baptists, of which the main ones were the same as those of Erbery noted above.[14]

In response to these arguments Knollys argued that the Calvinistic Baptists did not "judge it meet, for any Brother to baptise, or to administer other Ordinances; unless he have received such gifts of the Spirit, as fitteth, or enableth him to preach the Gospel. And those gifts being first tried by, and known to the Church, such a Brother is chosen, and appointed thereunto by the

Suffrage of the Church".[15] Those appointed by Calvinistic Baptist congregations to preach and administer the ordinances were not devoid of spiritual gifts. True, they did not have the same array of spiritual gifts as their first-century counterparts. But, Knollys went on to emphasise: "Such [extraordinary] gifts and miracles were rather for bringing the Word of the Gospel into the world, and for glorifying Christ's first coming in the flesh, than for after, Hebrews 2:3,4; John 20:29,30,31".[16] Knollys did not regard the miraculous gifts of the first-century church as vital to the life of the church in every age. These gifts were given to illuminate the entrance of the gospel onto the scene of history and to adorn the first advent of Christ. For biblical support he cited two texts: Hebrews 2:3-4, which clearly affirms the authenticating role of the spiritual gifts bestowed in the early church, and John 20:29-31, which also stresses the confirmatory role of miracles.

This line of argumentation was not new; it went back to Reformers like Martin Bucer (1491-1551) and John Calvin.[17] Knollys, moreover, maintained that the Baptists did find their proclamation of the gospel to be accompanied by miracles - miracles of regeneration. "So often as the Gospel comes to any Soul not in word only, but in power and in the Holy Spirit, 1 Thessalonians 1:5, there is a Miracle wrought in them that receive the Gospel, Luke 7:22, and they then receive the Holy Spirit with his gifts and graces ... So then we need not stay [i.e. wait] for a Ministry with Miracle, being we have a Word with Miracle".[18] Preaching that is empowered by the Spirit to the salvation of sinners is in itself miraculous. This perspective is fully in line with the Puritan thought of the day. The Puritan preacher Thomas Adams (fl. 1612-1653), for example, had stated:

> Even still God works miracles, though we take no notice of them. That our hearts should be converted, this is a miracle. That our faith should believe above reason, this is a miracle ... If he does not fetch water out of a rock, yet he fetcheth repentance out of sin, and makes the stony heart gush out tears; this is a greater miracle.[19]

Thus, Knollys concluded: "Although we have no gifts in our Churches but what we have received, and we have not received any Gifts of the Spirit to boast of them: Yet I must bear this Testimony, we come behind in no gift; what we have received we are bound to bless God for, and desire to honour Christ our Head with all the gifts which we have received from him".[20] Knollys and his fellow Baptists laid no claim to possessing all of the gifts which were present in the early church, but they were conscious nevertheless that the Spirit was at work among them through a variety of gifts.

Knollys' conviction with regard to the whole subject of spiritual gifts is especially instructive in our day when twentieth-century heirs of the Seekers maintain that the full panoply of the Spirit's gifts is always available to the church. Knollys was rightly unconvinced that post-New Testament believers had access to *all* of the spiritual gifts in evidence in the Apostolic era. Moreover, contrary to the views of the Seekers, Knollys did not believe that the absence of these gifts impeded the establishment of Spirit-filled congregations. The Spirit always gives that which the church needs. As Knollys' friend Benjamin Keach (1640-1704), another key Baptist leader in the latter half of the seventeenth century, wrote in a book which Knollys publicly commended: "Whilst there is a Church Militant, Saints on this side Perfection, ... those Spiritual Gifts needful to their present State, shall be given, and be amongst them, for the Support of the great Ordinance of the Ministry, and for the good of the Church".[21]

Noteworthy in the last text cited above from *The Shining of a Flaming Fire in Zion* is the Trinitarian emphasis that Knollys highlights: in the bestowal of the gifts of the Spirit, God the Father and Christ the Son are also vitally involved. Knollys had occasion to discuss further Christ's involvement in the bestowal of spiritual gifts in another work, *Christ Exalted*, a sermon on Colossians 3:11. Christ, Knollys affirmed, has purchased the gifts through his death, and as such is the "Alpha and Omega, the beginning and the ending, of all those graces, gifts, and fruits of the Spirit, which are in the new man". It is Christ who gives "lustre and beauty" to each spiritual gift. Indeed, it was the Father's design that "Christ should communicate all grace, gifts, etc. unto his people".[22] And because he is the source of the gifts, Christ is to be more highly prized than any of them.

In making this final point Knollys enunciated what will become a familiar theme in the Calvinistic Baptist tradition, namely, the subsidiary importance of the gifts of the Spirit in the Christian life.

Let Christ be all, in all in the gifts of the Spirit and graces of sanctification; for ... he is the Author, the Preserver, and finisher of them all. Therefore let him have the pre-eminence above all, set an high esteem of every gift and grace of God, account a little grace better than all the riches, honours, pleasures, and creature-comforts of this world. But you ought to prize Christ far above all his own gifts and graces in us, for he is the life of them all, the marrow and substance of them all. What is all knowledge, unless ye know God in Christ? 1 Corinthians 13:2: nothing. What is all faith, except Christ be the object of it? 1 Corinthians 13:2: nothing.[23]

Knollys was insistent that Christ is far more precious than any of his gifts. For possession of Christ is evidence of salvation, whereas that of the gifts is not. "If you have Christ, you have all ... but if you lose him you lose all; you will lose your hopes, Comforts, and all your duties, yea you will lose God, Heaven, and soul, and all. It matters not what you have if you want Christ, no gifts, duties, reformations, qualifications, or other things whatsoever, will make you happy without Christ. ... Therefore make sure that Christ is yours."[24] Knollys then proceeded to apply this perspective on the gifts of the Spirit to the age-old problem of believers being overawed by other, more gifted Christians.

Hear this you poor in spirit, you new-born babes in Christ, who have the persons of believers (especially Preachers) in admiration, and set them up on high in your hearts, and extol them with your tongues; because you discern so much humility, love, patience, faith, and other gifts of the Spirit, and graces of sanctification in them: should you not rather admire Christ, exalt Christ, and extol him, who is the purchaser, the owner, the donor, and the author of all these spiritual gifts and graces, for we have nothing but what we have received, by his grace we are what we are, and all the grace we have, from his freeness we received it, John 1:16. Therefore let him receive the glory of all, and let him have the pre-eminence in all, for he is all in all.[25]

This text well reveals the Christ-centred nature of early Calvinistic Baptist thought and worship. Christ, not his servants, is to be the object of the church's adoration.

Knollys and physical healing

During the grim years of persecution from the 1660s to the 1680s
Knollys was twice imprisoned, but, as has been mentioned, he
survived to see the dawn of a new era, when William III secured the
passing of the Toleration Act in 1689. Although Knollys' physical
capabilities appear to have been somewhat restricted, he and his
fellow Baptist William Kiffin took the occasion of this declaration
of toleration to issue a call for the first national assembly of
Calvinistic Baptists. The representatives of the one hundred or so
churches which met in London in September of 1689 gave their
formal assent to what is known as the *Second London Confession of
Faith*, the definitive Calvinistic Baptist Confession of the
seventeenth century. Attached to the Confession was a list of names,
thirty-seven Calvinistic Baptist pastors who concurred with the
Confession, and it was appropriate that heading the list was the name
of Knollys.

The same year that this assembly took place in London, Knollys
was involved in a fascinating event that is recorded by Thomas
Crosby in *The History of the English Baptists*. Crosby's father-in-
law was Benjamin Keach, who was taken ill in 1689 and was
expected to die. But, Crosby records: "The reverend Mr. Hanserd
Knollis[26] seeing his then dying friend, and brother in the Gospel,
near, to all appearance, expiring, betook himself to prayer, and in an
earnest and very extraordinary manner begged, that God would
spare him, and add unto his days, the time he granted to his servant
Hezekiah; and as soon as he had ended his prayer, he said, Brother
Keach I shall be in heaven before you, and quickly after left him".[27]
Knollys would die two years later; Keach lived another fifteen
years, dying in 1704, the same span of years God added to the life
of Hezekiah according to Isaiah 38.

How can this incident from Knollys' life be reconciled with his
clearly held belief that the extraordinary gifts of the Spirit were a
thing of the past? One answer, that given by Joseph Ivimey, is that
Knollys probably thought: "The direction given [in] James v.14-16,
was not confined to those who possessed the "gifts of healing", as
one of the extraordinary gifts of the Holy Spirit, bestowed in the
Apostolic times; but that it extended to all the ministers of Christ".[28]
A more general answer, building on that of Ivimey, would be that
while Knollys did not believe in the continuation of the

extraordinary gifts given to the first-century church, nor look for their restoration, neither did he wish to restrict the sovereignty of God and wholly confine his wondrous deeds to the past. God could and did still heal in answer to prayer. Knollys' position appears to be essentially the same as that of other Puritan authors. For instance, John Owen (1616-1683), the leading theologian of Restoration Puritanism, could state in *A Discourse of Spiritual Gifts*: "It is not unlikely but that God might on some occasions ... put forth his power in some miraculous operations; and so he yet may do and perhaps doth sometimes".[29]

Knollys died in 1691 when he was in his ninety-third year, a mature and "old disciple of Jesus Christ". To the end he retained his clarity of mind and solicitude for his flock, as a final letter to his church amply bears witness. After Knollys had especially commended the church in this letter "for continuing in the apostles' doctrine and fellowship, in breaking of bread, and in prayer", he went on to exhort his flock to be zealous in God's service and to have their zeal directed by "the light of knowledge" and the glory of God.[30] Well over a hundred years later this letter could call forth from an anonymous reviewer in *The Baptist Magazine* the desire that "the spirit which indited it be possessed in an abundant measure by all our Pastors".[31]

6.
The Second London Confession of Faith: **Its purpose**

When the Calvinistic Baptists met in London in 1689 for their first national assembly, the most significant decision from a historical perspective that they made was to undertake the publication of a confession of faith, the *Second London Confession of Faith*, which would become the classic expression of Calvinistic Baptist doctrine. As has already been noted in Chapter 4, however, this Confession had actually first seen the light of day twelve years earlier in 1677. In the preface which was attached to this Confession when it was first published, two explicit reasons for the publication of the new Confession were given. In the first place, the *First London Confession*, which had helped to satisfy many that the Calvinistic Baptists were in "no way guilty of those Heterodoxies and fundamental errors, which had too frequently been charged upon [them] without ground, or occasion given on [their] part", was "not now commonly to be had". Then, there were "many others" who had "embraced the same truth" which was set forth in the *First London Confession* and had presumably requested a compact expression of their faith.[1] Yet, it may be asked, why was the *First London Confession of Faith* not simply reprinted? To answer this question, it will be necessary to look at the events which intervened between the publication of the *First London Confession* and that of the *Second London Confession*.

Persecution

The *First London Confession of Faith* served the Calvinistic Baptists well during the 1640s and 1650s when the rule of Parliament and then that of Oliver Cromwell afforded them an unprecedented degree of freedom to evangelise and plant new churches. But, as we have noted, the return of Charles II to England in 1660 completely changed this situation. Persecution now became the order of the day. Interestingly enough, Charles II, who was a crypto-Roman Catholic and was received into the Roman Church on his deathbed, seems to have had a sincere desire for religious toleration. This desire probably stemmed from the fact that toleration would have given security to fellow Roman Catholics. But, as British historian Michael R. Watts has noted, "Though Charles wanted religious toleration, he wanted the crown more".[2] To keep his crown Charles needed Parliament, and the Parliament which came to power with Charles in 1660 had little sympathy for Puritanism either within or outside of the Church of England. Consequently, for the next twenty-eight years those who would not conform to the Church of England were subjected to "calculated and often malicious persecution".[3] For instance, in June of 1662, the Petty France Calvinistic Baptist Church in London was attacked by a group of soldiers, who, one record states, "came to Petty France full of Rage and Violence, with their Swords drawn; they wounded some, and struck others, broke down the Gallery, and made much spoil".[4]

Of course, the Calvinistic Baptists were not the only ones to suffer during this time of great persecution; all who dissented from the rites and practices of the Church of England suffered to one degree or another. This furnace of common affliction only served to reinforce in the minds of many Calvinistic Baptists just how much they shared with fellow Calvinists who were either Presbyterians or Congregationalists, the latter being then known as Independents. Moreover, there was at hand a document which could concretely demonstrate the essential doctrinal unity between these three groups, namely, the *Westminster Confession of Faith*. This Confession, the authoritative statement of faith of both the Church of Scotland and the English Presbyterians, had been issued by the Westminster Assembly in 1646. The Independents had subsequently used it as the basis of their statement of faith, known as the *Savoy Declaration*, which was drawn up in 1658 by such leading Puritan authors as John Owen and Thomas Goodwin (1600-1680).[5] The desire to present a united Calvinist front in the face of persecution consequently led the Calvinistic Baptists to employ the *Westminster Confession*, as modified by the *Savoy Declaration*, as the basis of a new Confession.[6]

Hyper-Calvinism

A second reason for a new confession was the appearance of Hyper-Calvinism in the south-west of England. Andrew Gifford, Sr. (1642-1721), pastor of the Pithay Calvinistic Baptist Church in Bristol, knew "some ministers who were of the opinion that as none could pray acceptably without the influences of the Holy Spirit, and unconverted men being destitute of those influences, that therefore it was not their duty to pray, nor the duty of ministers to exhort them to seek for spiritual blessings".[7] Gifford wrote to the Baptist pastors in London seeking their opinion on the matter.

A letter was drawn up in January of 1675 by William Kiffin and a number of other London Baptists, in which it was unequivocally stated that "prayer is a part of that homage which every man is obliged to give to God" and that it is "a duty belonging to natural, and not only to instituted religion". Support for this position was found in Acts 17:26-27, where the apostle Paul declared to the Athenian philosophers on the Areopagus that God has so ordered the history of the world that men and women "should seek the Lord". As Kiffin and his fellow Baptists went on to note: "Whatever in that text is meant by seeking, prayer cannot (by any just reason) be excluded; and if prayer be intended, 'tis comprehensive of all mankind. It cannot be supposed that man, being such a creature as he is, should not be obliged to love, fear, and obey God". In response to the objection that "such persons have not the Spirit, [and] therefore ought not to pray", the London Baptists were unequivocal in their reply.

> This objection is not cogent, forasmuch as neither the want of the Spirit's immediate motions to, or its assistance in the duty, doth not take off the obligation to the duty. If it would, then also, from every other duty; and consequently all religion would be cashiered. If the obligation to this and other duties were suspended merely for want of such motions or assistance, then unconverted persons are so far from sinning in the omission of such duties, that it is their duty to omit them. 'Tis certain no man can, without the assistance of the Holy Spirit, either repent or believe; yet it

will not therefore follow, that impenitency and unbelief are no sins; if these be sins, then the contrary must be their duty.[8]

Coming only a couple of years before the publication of the *Second London Confession*, this issue was certain to be on the minds of those who compiled this Confession.

The threat of the Quakers

Yet another reason which prompted the desire to issue a new confession was the threat posed by the Quakers.[9] The Quaker movement had started in the late 1640s when George Fox (1624-1691), a shoemaker and part-time shepherd, began to win converts to a perspective on the Christian faith which rejected much of orthodox Puritan theology. Fox and the early Quakers proclaimed the possibility of salvation for all humanity, and urged men and women to turn to the light within them to find salvation. We "call All men to look to the Light within their own consciences," wrote Samuel Fisher (1605-1665), a General Baptist turned Quaker; "by the leadings of that Light ... they may come to God, and work out their Salvation."[10] This emphasis on the light within, which the Quakers variously called the indwelling Christ or Spirit, often led them to elevate it above the Scriptures.

For the Puritans, including the Calvinistic Baptists, the nature of the Spirit's work in the authors of Scripture was unique and definitely a thing of the past. The Spirit was now *illuminating* that which he had inspired and their experiences of the Spirit were to be tried by the Scriptures. As Richard Baxter (1615-1691), a moderate Puritan author, declared:

We must not try the Scriptures by our most spiritual apprehensions, but our apprehensions by the Scriptures: that is, we must prefer the Spirit's inspiring the apostles to indite the Scriptures before the Spirit's illuminating of us to understand them, or before any present inspirations, the former being the more perfect; because Christ gave the apostles the Spirit to deliver us infallibly his own commands, and to indite a rule for following ages:

but he giveth us the Spirit but to understand and use that rule aright. This trying the Spirit by the Scriptures is not a setting of the Scriptures above the Spirit itself; but it is only a trying of the Spirit by the Spirit; that is, the Spirit's operations in themselves and his revelations to any pretenders now, by the Spirit's operations in the apostles and by their revelations recorded for our use.[11]

With the Quakers, though, there was a deep conviction that the Spirit was speaking in them as he had spoken in the apostles. In practice, this often led to an elevation of their experience of the indwelling Spirit over the Scriptures. Thus, when some Baptists in Huntingdonshire and Cambridgeshire became Quakers and declared that the "light in their consciences was the rule they desire to walk by", not the Scriptures, they were simply expressing what was implicit in the entire Quaker movement.[12]

This desire to live by what they regarded as the dictates of the indwelling Spirit rather than by the written Word sometimes led the early Quakers into quite bizarre patterns of behaviour. Probably the oddest was the practice of "going naked as a sign"![13] One Quaker who appears to have been something of an "expert" in this type of behaviour was Solomon Eccles (*ca.* 1618-1683). When he first went naked in 1659 he asserted that he did so because by "the same spirit [which moved Isaiah and Ezekiel] hath the Lord raised me up, to go as a Sign to this dark Generation". While the practice of "going naked as a sign" was a relatively infrequent occurrence after 1662 - though Eccles was still engaged in it as late as 1669 - the phenomenon reveals the tendency inherent in Quakerism to exalt the Spirit at the expense of the Word.

Isaac Penington the Younger (1616-1679) is one early Quaker author who well illustrates this tendency to make the indwelling Spirit rather than the Scriptures the touchstone and final authority for thought and practice. Converted to Quakerism in 1658 after hearing George Fox preach the previous year, Penington became an important figure in the movement. In the words of J. W. Frost, Penington "remains a prime example of the intellectual sophistication of the second generation of Quaker converts".[14] In a letter that he wrote a fellow Quaker by the name of Nathanael Stonar in 1670,

Penington told his correspondent that one of the main differences between themselves and other "professors" was "concerning *the rule*". While the latter asserted that the Scriptures were the rule by which men and women ought to direct their lives and thinking, Penington was convinced that the indwelling Spirit of life is "nearer and more powerful, than the words, or outward relations concerning those things in the Scriptures". As Penington noted:

> The Lord, in the gospel state, hath promised to be present with his people; not as a wayfaring man, for a night, but to *dwell in them and walk in them*. Yea, if they be tempted and in danger of erring, they shall hear a voice behind them, saying, "This is the way, walk in it." Will they not grant this to be a rule, as well as the Scriptures? Nay, is not this a more full direction to the heart, in that state, than it can pick to itself out of the Scriptures? ... the Spirit, which gave forth the words, is greater than the words; therefore we cannot but prize Him himself, and set Him higher in our heart and thoughts, than the words which testify of Him, though they also are very sweet and precious to our taste.[15]

Penington here affirmed that the Quakers esteemed the Scriptures as "sweet and precious". but he was equally adamant that the indwelling Spirit was to be regarded as the supreme authority when it came to direction for Christian living and thinking.[16]

The Quakers especially preyed on Baptist congregations, shattering many of them in the process of winning converts. While the General Baptists were more susceptible to the views of the Quakers, the Particular Baptists were by no means immune. For instance, a member of the Petty France Particular Baptist Church, a Sister Hattam, was, after being admonished, excommunicated in October of 1676 for joining the Quakers. Another good example is Luke Howard, who was instrumental in persuading Samuel Fisher to become a Quaker. Howard had been baptised by William Kiffin in either 1643 or 1644, but subsequently went over to the Quakers.[17] In the West Country, several leading Quakers had been Baptists prior to their change of mind. Thomas Budd, known once as a "Baptist teacher", opened up his property for large Quaker

gatherings. William Ames, who had been a Baptist minister in
Somerset, became a Quaker while serving as a soldier in Ireland.
Jasper Batt (d. 1702), who later preached at George Fox's funeral,
had also once been a Baptist.[18] To help minimise such Calvinistic
Baptist losses to the Quakers, it was clear that a more comprehensive
statement on the nature of the authority of Scripture was needed than
the various remarks found here and there in the *First London
Confession*.

The doctrinal defection of Thomas Collier

Possibly the most pressing doctrinal reason for a new confession
was the defection of Thomas Collier (fl.1634?-1691).[19] Collier, a
member of William Kiffin's church, had served as a chaplain with
the parliamentary troops in the final years of the Civil War. In 1651
he became an itinerant evangelist in the south-west of England,
where he laboured for the next fifteen years. During this period he
became a well-known leader among the Calvinistic Baptists.
Testimony to Collier's importance comes from Thomas Edwards
(1599-1647), a Presbyterian and Puritan in theology, but one who
had a deep-seated antipathy towards the Baptists. He described
Collier thus: "This Collier is a great sectary in the west of England,
a mechanical fellow [i.e. a vulgar fellow belonging to the lower
classes], and a great emissary, a dipper who goes about Surrey,
Hampshire, and those countries, preaching and dipping".[20]

In 1674, however, Collier published a work entitled *A Body of
Divinity*, which sent shock-waves throughout the Calvinistic
Baptist community, for in this book Collier denied the Calvinistic
doctrine of original sin, argued that Christ had died for all men and
women, and maintained that Christ's humanity was eternal.[21] Due to
Collier's standing among the Calvinistic Baptists it was imperative
that his views be dealt with. A meeting was arranged between
Collier and five Baptist ministers from London, including Kiffin
and Nehemiah Coxe, who was one of the pastors of the Petty France
Calvinistic Baptist Church.[22] Collier, though, refused to renounce
his new views and he was duly accused of heresy. Although Coxe
published an extensive rebuttal of Collier's views in 1677, the
controversy threatened to call into question the commitment of the

Calvinistic Baptists to Calvinism. A fresh statement of their commitment to Calvinism was needed.

Publication of the Confession

The new confession was issued in 1677. Although it was published anonymously, it appears that it was prepared by Coxe and his fellow pastor William Collins.[23] Collins had studied in France and Italy, and taken a B. D. in England. Efforts were made to induce him into conforming to the Church of England, but he resisted them and in 1675 he accepted a call to pastor the Petty France Church. Coxe had originally been a member of John Bunyan's church in Bedford, had spent time with Bunyan in prison for preaching the gospel, and had been ordained to the ministry at the same church meeting which called Bunyan to be the pastor of the church.[24]

As has been noted, Collins and Coxe used the *Westminster Confession* and the *Savoy Declaration* in their preparation of the *Second London Confession*. Nevertheless, they did not reproduce these confessions holus-bolus. As they stated in the preface: "Some things, indeed, are in some places added, some terms omitted, and some few changed."[25] These changes relate to not only such obvious things as baptism and church government, but also include modification in other less obvious areas. The treatment of reprobation, for example, in both the *Westminster Confession* and the *Savoy Declaration* describes the reprobate as being "foreordained to everlasting death". The *Second London Confession* softens this somewhat by stating that the reprobate are "left to act in their sin to their just condemnation".[26] Moreover, in the same article an entire paragraph on reprobation which is found in the *Westminster Confession* and the *Savoy Declaration* has been deleted from the *Second London Confession*. Another change appears in the article relating to worship. In the *Westminster Confession* and the *Savoy Declaration* singing is restricted to the "singing of psalms". But in the *Second London Confession* "Hymns and Spiritual Songs" are included alongside the Psalms as fit material for singing.[27] Yet, as Robert Oliver notes: "These differences must not be allowed to obscure the overwhelming agreement between the *Second London Confession* and those of

Westminster and *Savoy*. The Baptist Confession can be clearly seen to be in the stream of evangelical theology, which flowed from the Westminster Assembly".[28]

As we have seen, twelve years after the publication of the *Second London Confession* in 1677 it was issued again by the first national assembly of Calvinistic Baptists as the "confession we own, as containing the doctrine of our faith and practice".[29] In the following chapter we look at three aspects of that doctrine, those relating to Scripture, Calvinist soteriology, and the Lord's Supper in the hope that the *Second London Confession* might be appreciated not only as an historical document but also be seen as a relevant guide for the Christian life today.

7.
The Second London Confession of Faith: Its Theology

A high view of Scripture

Following the order of the *Westminster Confession* and the *Savoy Declaration*, the *Second London Confession of Faith* begins with a lengthy chapter on Scripture. In the words of the American Baptist authors L. Ross Bush and Tom J. Nettles, this chapter "contains the clearest confessional statement on Scripture in all of Christendom".[1] Apart from an introductory sentence and a concluding phrase it virtually reproduces the parallel chapters of the *Westminster Confession* and the *Savoy Declaration*. The introductory sentence, though, is highly significant and a valuable gauge as to where the seventeenth-century Calvinistic Baptists stood with regard to the nature of Scripture.

"The Holy Scripture", it states, "is the only sufficient, certain, and infallible rule of all saving Knowledge, Faith, and Obedience".[2] This sentence describes the nature of Scripture by four carefully chosen terms. The first term, "only", emphasises that apart from the Scriptures there is no other source of ultimate religious authority. Further on in its statement on Scripture, the *Second London Confession* elaborates on this claim by stating that nothing is to be added to Scripture, "whether by new revelations of the Spirit, or traditions of men".[3] In the historical context of the Confession this statement would especially rule out the revelations of the Quakers, which their opponents felt were being elevated to authoritative status alongside Scripture.

Then this opening sentence of the Confession asserts that, while God does reveal himself in ways other than the Scriptures, for instance through the created realm, only Scripture is "sufficient" to "give that knowledge of God and his will which is necessary unto salvation".[4] Or in the words of the *Second London Confession* 1.6: "The whole Counsel of God concerning all things necessary for his own Glory, Man's Salvation, Faith and Life, is either expressly set down or necessarily contained in the Holy Scripture".[5] The written Scriptures are necessary for God to be properly glorified by men and women, as well as being vital for men and women to come to a saving knowledge of God, and then to develop a world-view (so Bush and Nettles interpret "faith"[6]) and lifestyle that is in accord with their salvation.

The next two terms of the opening sentence of this article on Scripture are similar, but not identical, in their import. Scripture is "certain", that is, it does not contain error. Bush and Nettles consider this term to be equivalent to the word "inerrant" as it is currently used in evangelical circles to mean that which is totally truthful. Scripture is also said to be "infallible", a term that has a long history of usage in Christian theology, and which identifies Scripture as possessing the quality of being entirely trustworthy and reliable.[7]

Given the very real threat posed by the Quaker movement to Calvinistic Baptist churches, it seems most probable that the strengthening of this statement on Scripture is a definite response to this situation. In their emphasis on Scripture as the supreme arbiter for the Christian life, the Calvinistic Baptists were reflecting their Puritan heritage, for "Puritanism was first and foremost a movement centred in Scripture".[8] Thus, from the Calvinistic Baptist point of view, the Quakers were guilty of making an unbiblical cleavage between the Spirit and the Word. As Benjamin Keach declared in 1681, in a direct allusion to the Quakers: "Many are confident they have the Spirit, Light, and Power, when 'tis all mere Delusion. The Spirit always leads and directs according to the written Word: "He shall bring my Word," saith Christ, "to your remembrance" [cf. John 14:26]".[9]

Lest it be thought that the seventeenth-century Calvinistic Baptists, in their desire to emphasise the authority of the Scriptures, went to the opposite extreme and depreciated the importance of the work of the Spirit in the Christian life, one needs to note the words of the *Second London Confession* 1.5, where it is stated that "our full persuasion, and assurance of the infallible truth" of the Scriptures comes neither from "the testimony of the Church of God" nor from the "heavenliness of the matter" of the Scriptures, the "efficacy of [their] Doctrine", and "the Majesty of [their] Stile". Rather it is only "the inward work of the Holy Spirit, bearing witness by and with the Word in our Hearts" that convinces believers that God's Word is indeed what it claims to be.[10]

In the Reformed heritage

In light of the documents that were used in the preparation of the *Second London Confession*, as well as some of the reasons for its publication, it is only to be expected that the distinguishing tenets of Calvinism are highly visible in the Confession. Each of what are described as "the five points of Calvinism" is treated clearly and comprehensively. Now, an excellent window for observing the Calvinism of the *Second London Confession* is its doctrine of the work of the Holy Spirit.

It was Benjamin B. Warfield, the early twentieth-century Presbyterian theologian, who once stated that the greatest contribution of John Calvin, the spiritual father of the Calvinistic Baptists, to the science of theology was his systematic exposition of the work of the Holy Spirit. In Warfield's words, it was Calvin "who first related the whole experience of salvation specifically to the working of the Holy Spirit, worked it out into its details, and contemplated its several steps and stages in orderly progress as the product of the Holy Spirit's specific work in applying salvation to the soul. Thus he gave systematic and adequate expression to the whole doctrine of the Holy Spirit and made it the assured possession of the Church of God".[11] And of Calvin's theological heirs, it was especially the Puritans who shared this great interest of the French Reformer.[12] It is thus quite appropriate to examine the Calvinism of the *Second London Confession* through its discussion of the work of the Holy Spirit in salvation.[13]

For a man or woman to repent and turn to God, it is necessary that there be a prior work of the Spirit. As the *Second London Confession* 10.1-2 puts it:

> Those whom God hath predestined unto Life, he is pleased, in his appointed, and accepted time, effectually to call by his word, and Spirit, out of that state of sin, and death, in which they are by nature, to grace and Salvation by Jesus Christ; enlightening their minds, spiritually, and savingly to understand the things of God; taking away their heart of stone, and giving unto them an heart of flesh; renewing their wills, and by his Almighty power determining them to that which is good, and effectually drawing them to Jesus Christ; yet so as they come most freely, being made willing by his Grace.[14]

Due to the fact that those outside of Christ are dead spiritually, blind to the things of God, unresponsive to his appeals, and in bondage to sin, God has to undertake on their behalf if they are ever to be saved. This he does for those sinners he has elected to save by re-modelling their wills and giving them new affections. In the same action, God quickens them and gives them new life through his Spirit. They are now able to respond to God and embrace all that Christ has done for them.

The same truth is emphasised in a later article entitled "Of the Gospel, and of the extent of the Gospel thereof". This article is not to be found in the *Westminster Confession*, but appears first in the *Savoy Declaration*, which is the source for its inclusion in the *Second London Confession*.[15] In the fourth paragraph of this article we read that "although the Gospel be the only outward means, of revealing Christ, and saving grace; and is, as such, abundantly sufficient thereunto; yet that men who are dead in Trespasses, may be born again, Quickened or Regenerated; there is moreover necessary, an effectual, insuperable work of the Holy Spirit, upon the whole Soul, for the producing in them a new spiritual Life; without which no other means will effect their Conversion unto God".[16] For a person to be converted it is not enough for him or her simply to hear the gospel and seek to respond to it in his or her own strength. Positive response to the gospel can only come about when the Spirit works with unconquerable power in the heart of the unbeliever, irresistibly giving to him or her the ability to turn to God.

Passages like Ezekiel 36:26-27 ("A new heart also will I give you, and a new spirit will I put within you: and I will take away the stony heart out of your flesh, and I will give you a heart of flesh. And I will put my Spirit within you, and cause you to walk in my statutes, and ye shall keep my judgments, and do them,") KJV led those who issued this Confession to see that God has promised "to give unto all those that are ordained unto eternal Life, his Holy Spirit, to make them willing, and able to believe".[17] It should come as no surprise, therefore, that saving faith is also recognised by the Confession to be the work of the Spirit. "The Grace of Faith," we read in Article 14, paragraph 1, "whereby the Elect are enabled to believe to the saving of their souls, is the work of the Spirit of Christ in their hearts".[18]

In this connection, it is also noteworthy that the *Second London Confession* emphasises a close link between the Spirit's work in salvation and the Word of God. Effectual calling, for instance, is by the "Word and Spirit". Also the "Grace of Faith", described above as a "work of the Spirit of Christ" in the heart, is normally given through "the Ministry of the Word".[19]

Furthermore, those whom the Spirit regenerates he also sanctifies: "They who are united to Christ, Effectually called, and regenerated, having a new heart, and a new Spirit created in them, through the virtue of Christ's death, and Resurrection; are also farther sanctified, really, and personally, through the same virtue, by his word and Spirit dwelling in them". The Confession especially emphasises that in this life, the sanctification of any believer is "yet imperfect", since within every child of God there is "a continual, and irreconcilable war; the Flesh lusting against the Spirit, and the Spirit against the Flesh", a clear reference to Paul's word in Galatians 5:17. Though the flesh or "the remaining corruption for a time may much prevail; yet through the continual supply of strength from the sanctifying Spirit of Christ the regenerate part doth overcome."[20] In other words, despite setbacks and failures the ultimate outcome of the believer's struggle against the flesh will be victory for the believer. But such a victory is only possible because of the power given to the believer by the indwelling Holy Spirit.

This perspective on the Christian life was essentially that of the Puritans. John Owen, for instance, in a series of sermons on Romans 8:13, had argued that the believer has a constant duty to engage in putting to death the sin that still indwells his or her mortal frame. But such a duty is only possible in the strength supplied by the Holy Spirit, who alone is "sufficient for this work".[21] An earlier Puritan author, Richard Sibbes (1577-1635), could state that to those whom God forgives, "he gives his Spirit to sanctify them. The same Spirit that assures me of the pardon of my sin, sanctifies my nature".[22] Owen's argument, Sibbes' comment and the paragraph from the Baptist Confession stand as a proper corrective to those evangelical quarters today which maintain that regeneration need not be followed by sanctification, that one can, in popular parlance, have Jesus as one's Saviour and not as one's Lord. The early Calvinistic Baptists, like the Puritan movement out of which it had sprung, would have regarded such sentiments as both misguided and unbiblical. Those in whom the Spirit works saving faith he comes to indwell, and as the indwelling Holy Spirit he never abides without his holy and moral character reshaping the lives of those in whom he dwells.[23]

The Confession goes on to indicate that the Spirit, along with the Father and Son, is vitally involved in enabling believers to persevere in the faith. "Those whom God hath accepted in the beloved", we read in the *Second London Confession* 17.1, 2, "effectually called and Sanctified by his [i.e. God's] Spirit, and given the precious faith of his Elect unto, can neither totally nor finally fall from the state of grace; but shall certainly persevere therein to the end and be eternally saved". The believer's perseverance ultimately depends not on the exercise of his or her own free will, but, among other things, upon "the abiding of his [i.e. God's] Spirit & the seed of God within" the believer.[24]

Perseverance ultimately issues in glorification; and here too, the Confession indicates, the Holy Spirit is active. As it states in chapter 31:3: "The bodies of the unjust shall by the power of Christ be raised to dishonour; the bodies of the just by his Spirit unto honour".[25] The text to which the Confession turns to justify its inclusion of "by his Spirit" here is Philippians 3:21, The Lord Jesus Christ "shall" change our vile body, that it may be fashioned like unto his glorious body, according to the working whereby he is able even to subdue all things unto himself" (KJV), a verse which contains no explicit mention of the Spirit. Evidently those who issued the Confession understood the phrase "according to the working" as an oblique reference to the Holy Spirit. Probably a better proof text at this point would have been Romans 8:11, where the Holy Spirit's involvement in the resurrection of believers is clearly indicated.

It should be pointed out that this sturdy Calvinism of the *Second London Confession* is also a firmly evangelical Calvinism. For instance, in chapter 7.2 it is stated unequivocally that "Man having brought himself under the curse of the Law by his fall, it pleased the Lord to make a Covenant of Grace wherein he freely offereth unto Sinners, Life and Salvation by Jesus Christ, requiring of them Faith in him, that they may be saved".[26] The statement that God "freely offereth unto Sinners, Life and Salvation by Jesus Christ" envisages an unencumbered preaching of the gospel to all and sundry.[27] Numerous statements could be culled from the writings of those who issued this Confession which make the same point. For instance, Hanserd Knollys could state unambiguously:

> The ordinarie meanes which God hath in his infinite
> wisdom appointed to convert sinners, and also to build

them up in Christ, is the Word preached, Rom. 10:8, 17. This word of the Gospel God will have preached to every creature in all parts of [the] world, Mark 16:15. None are exempted or prohibited from hearing the Gospel preached, but everyone that hath an eare is required to heare, Rev. 2:7.[28]

And Benjamin Keach maintained that the Holy Spirit is "a River that lieth open to all poor Sinners; whoever will may come to these Waters", and that "Christ is sent to all, to Jews and Gentiles, to the Small as well as the Great, to the Poor as well as the Rich; none are excluded".[29]

In the following century a significant number of Calvinistic Baptist preachers would reject this aspect of the Confession. Embracing Hyper-Calvinism, they would have little or nothing to say to the unconverted. Their view of salvation cut the nerve of aggressive Baptist evangelism, and not surprisingly led to a neglect of the *Second London Confession*. There were new editions of the Confession up until the fifth edition in 1720. But no new edition appeared after that point until 1791. As Robert Oliver has noted: "This long eclipse of a Confession, which had received the commendation of a representative Assembly in 1689, creates the suspicion that its theology was not completely acceptable for much of the eighteenth century".[30] It is noteworthy, though, that new editions of the Confession began to appear when revival came to the Calvinistic Baptists at the end of the eighteenth century, and when evangelical Calvinism was once again widely embraced as biblical Calvinism by this Baptist community.

The Lord's Supper

The chapter in the Confession dealing with the Lord's Supper, chapter 30, is a good example of the way in which the Calvinistic Baptists sought to demonstrate their fundamental solidarity with other Calvinists. Following the *Westminster Confession* and the *Savoy Declaration*, the Baptist Confession denounces as unbiblical the Roman Church's doctrine of the mass, its practice of private masses, its refusal to allow any but a priest to partake of the cup, and its dogma of transubstantiation.[31] Having noted such errors regarding the Lord's Table, a right understanding of this ordinance is then inculcated. "Worthy receivers, outwardly partaking of the visible Elements in this Ordinance, do then also inwardly by faith, really and indeed, yet not carnally, and corporally, but spiritually receive, and feed upon Christ crucified & all the benefits of his death: the Body and Blood of Christ, being then not corporally, or carnally, but spiritually present to the faith of Believers, in that Ordinance, as the Elements themselves are to their outward senses".[32] Close comparison of this statement with the parallel statements in the *Westminster Confession* and the *Savoy Declaration* reveals two main areas of difference. The two earlier confessions use the term "sacrament" to describe the Lord's Supper, whereas in the *Second London Confession* this has been altered to "ordinance".[33] Neither term is actually used in the New Testament, but the term "ordinance" appears to have been adopted to stress the divine institution of the Lord's Supper.[34]

The second change is an omission. The omission is best seen by displaying the relevant passages side by side in the following table, with the omitted words in italics.

Westminister Confession/ Savoy Declaration [35]	**Second London Confession** [36]
The body and blood of Christ being then not corporally or carnally, *in, with, or under the bread and wine, yet, as really*, but spiritually present to the faith of believers in the ordinance, as the faith of believers in that ordinance, as the elements themselves are to their outward senses.	The Body and Blood of Christ being then not corporally, or carnally, but spiritually present to the faith of Believers in that Ordinance, as the Elements themselves are to their outward senses.

The phrase which has been omitted in the *Second London Confession* was intended to reject the Lutheran explanation of how Christ is present in the Lord's Supper.[37] In the view of Martin Luther, Christ's body and blood are present "in, with, or under" the bread and the wine. Contrary to the Roman dogma of transubstantiation, the bread remains bread; yet, in some way, it also contains Christ's body after the prayer of consecration. Likewise the wine is his blood, but remains wine. Why the *Second London Confession* omits this phrase is not at all clear. Possibly Luther's view was not entertained by any in the Calvinistic Baptist community during the seventeenth century, and it was thus omitted so as to avoid encumbering the Confession with needless statements.

The differences between the three confessions, however, are minimal compared to what they have in common. All three affirm that as believers partake of the bread and the wine, they are actually feeding upon Christ crucified. Contrary to the dogma of the Roman Church, this feeding does not entail eating the physical body of Christ and drinking his physical blood. It is a spiritual feeding; Christ is "spiritually present" to believers in the Lord's Supper.

What did those who approved this Confession understand by this expression "spiritually present"? One of those who gave his approval to the Confession was Hercules Collins (d.1702), pastor of Wapping Baptist Church in London, who was a key Baptist leader in the capital and much in demand as a preacher. According to John Piggott, who preached his funeral sermon: "If he had not some men's accuracy, yet it was made up by a constant flame: for no man could preach with a more affectionate regard to the salvation of souls".[38] In his *An Orthodox Catechism* (1680) Collins stated that in the Lord's Supper we are "verily Partakers of his Body and Blood through the working of the Holy Ghost".[39] From Collins' perspective it is the Holy Spirit who makes Christ present in the Lord's Supper. Although Christ's body is in heaven, through the Spirit we can have communion with the risen Christ. Again, William Kiffin, in his response to John Bunyan in their debate over the question of open and closed communion, could state that "the [Lord's] Supper is a Spiritual participation of the Body and Blood of Christ by Faith".[40]

These views are essentially those of John Calvin. G. S. M. Walker has summarised Calvin's view of Christ's presence in the Supper thus: "Although communion is a spiritual act, it involves an actual sharing in Christ's flesh and blood, and although his body has now ascended physically into heaven, we are none the less able to make contact with it through the Spirit. How these things can be remains a mystery, to be treated with reverence and accepted in faith".[41] The Calvinistic Baptist Confession shares Calvin's perspective to the full. When it declares that Christ is "spiritually present" in the Lord's Supper, it is maintaining that Christ's presence in the Supper is one that is effected by the Holy Spirit.

A more detailed discussion of the importance of the Lord's Supper for the Christian life is provided in the first paragraph of chapter 30. There it is stated that the "Supper of the Lord Jesus was instituted by him, the same night wherein he was betrayed, to be observed in his Churches unto the end of the world, for the perpetual remembrance, and shewing forth the sacrifice in his death, confirmation of the faith of believers in all the benefits thereof, their spiritual nourishment, and growth in him, their further ingagement in, and to, all duties which they owe unto him; and to be a bond and pledge of their communion with him, and with each other".[42] In this enumeration of the reasons for the Lord's Table the *Second London Confession* follows closely the *Westminster Confession* and the *Savoy Declaration*. Christ instituted the Lord's Supper for five reasons according to this paragraph. The Supper serves as a vivid reminder of and witness to the sacrificial death of Christ. Then, participation in the Lord's Supper enables believers to grasp more firmly all that Christ has done for them through his death on the cross. In this way the Lord's Supper is a means of spiritual nourishment and growth. Fourth, the Lord's Supper serves as a time when believers can recommit themselves to Christ. Finally, the Lord's Supper affirms the indissoluble union which exists, on the one hand, between Christ and believers, and, on the other, between individual believers.

One cannot come away from reading these paragraphs on the Lord's Supper without the conviction that those who issued this Confession were deeply conscious of the importance of the Lord's Supper for the Christian life. Benjamin Keach speaks for his fellow Baptists when he states, probably with reference to the Quakers, who had discarded the observance of both baptism and the Lord's Supper: "Some men boast of the Spirit, and conclude they have the Spirit, and none but they, and yet at the same time cry down and vilify his blessed Ordinances and Institutions, which he hath left in his Word, carefully to be observed and kept ... The Spirit hath its Bounds, and always run[s] in its spiritual Channel, viz. the Word and Ordinances".[43]

In this hearty appreciation of the Lord's Supper these early Baptists were once again in the mainstream of Puritan thought. The Puritans generally regarded the Supper as a vehicle which the Spirit employed as an efficacious means of grace for the believer. And for the most part they opposed the view associated with the name of the Swiss Reformer Ulrich Zwingli, which looks upon the bread and the wine as simply signs and the Supper as chiefly a memorial.[44] In recent discussions of Zwingli's perspective on the Lord's Supper it is often maintained that Zwingli was not really a Zwinglian, that is, he saw more in the Lord's Supper than simply a memorial.[45] Be this as it may, a tradition did take its start from aspects of his thought, which stresses primarily the memorial nature of the Lord's Supper. In Calvinistic Baptist circles, this Zwinglian perspective on the Lord's Supper would eventually come to be the overwhelming consensus in the late eighteenth and nineteenth centuries. And it would be forgotten that the early Calvinistic Baptists were of quite a different mind. The seventeenth-century Baptists would have judged the Zwinglian view of the Lord's Supper as far too mean a perspective on what was for them such a rich means of grace. Indeed, in seeking to articulate a more balanced view of the Lord's Table, contemporary Baptists can do no better than to listen afresh to what their Baptist forebears wrote in chapter 30 of the *Second London Confession*.

Conclusion

The *Second London Confession* is certainly not perfect,[46] but it has much to teach twentieth-century Baptists, as the preceding discussion of certain doctrinal aspects of the Confession has hopefully shown. The comments of C. H. Spurgeon with regard to the Confession's usefulness, made when he republished it in 1855, are still relevant. "This little volume is not issued as an authoritative rule, or code of faith, whereby you are to be fettered, but as an assistance to you in controversy, a confirmation in faith, and a means of edification in righteousness. ...Cleave fast to the Word of God which is here mapped out for you".[47]

Benjamin Keach (1640-1704)

8.
Benjamin Keach (1640-1704), Baptist Divine

In a recently published history of religion in Britain Michael Mullett has identified Benjamin Keach as the leading Baptist theologian of his era, similar in importance for his denomination as Richard Baxter was for the English Presbyterians, John Owen for the Congregationalists and Robert Barclay (1648-1690) for the Quakers.[1] Mullett may well be drawing upon an earlier description of Keach by Murdina D. MacDonald: "the single most important apologist for Calvinistic Baptist views" in the final decade of the seventeenth century was the way that MacDonald had described Keach in her 1982 Oxford D. Phil. thesis. There were, of course, other important Baptist authors in this period - men such as Hercules Collins and Joseph Stennett (1663-1713), the pastor of a congregation that met in Pinners' Hall, London - but "neither the scope nor extent of their works matched Keach's production".[2] He argued against the Quakers and took to task fellow Puritans - notably Richard Baxter and John Flavel (*ca.* 1630-1691) - who defended infant baptism; he advocated the practice of laying on of hands at the time of baptism, a rite that was common amongst the General Baptists but rarely practised among the Calvinistic Baptists[3]; he wrote allegories, now long forgotten, that in his day rivalled those of John Bunyan in popularity and sales; he defended at length the singing of hymns and even compiled some of his own; he published a number of collections of sermons, including *A Golden Mine Opened* (1694) and *Gospel Mysteries Unveiled* (1701), which remain invaluable, though largely unused, treasures for the study of seventeenth-century Baptist thought[4]; and he penned the first Calvinistic Baptist treatise specifically devoted to ecclesiastical polity, *The Glory of a True Church, and its Doctrine display'd* (1697).

Early years

Keach was born on February 29, 1640 to John and Fedora Keach, an
Anglican couple residing at the time in Stoke Hammond, north
Buckinghamshire.[5] Raised an Anglican, he joined the General
Baptists when he was but fifteen. Within three years of his baptism
as a believer he was called to preach by the General Baptist
congregation that met in Winslow, Buckinghamshire, not far from
Stoke Hammond. There is still in existence in Winslow an old
Baptist meeting house dating from 1695 which is called Keach's
Meeting House. Whether or not Keach ever worshipped in this old
chapel is not known. Yet, it is an appropriate way to recall the
connection of this great Baptist leader with this area of
Buckinghamshire.[6]

Around the same time as his call to the ministry of the Word
Keach married Jane Grove (d. 1670), a native of Winslow. During
the ten or so years of their marriage the couple had five children, of
whom three survived infancy. One of them, Hannah, later became
a Quaker, which would have caused her father some distress. His
only surviving son from this marriage, Elias Keach (1667-1701),
would play a key rôle in advancing the Baptist cause in and around
Philadelphia in America.

As we have already noted, the 1660s through to the 1680s were
a time of great persecution for any who sought to worship outside
of the Church of England, and Keach found himself in trouble with
the state on more than one occasion. For instance, in 1664 he was
arrested on a charge of being "a seditious, heretical and schismatical
person, evilly and maliciously disposed and disaffected to his
Majesty's government and the government of the Church of
England".[7] It appears that a children's primer which Keach had
written containing reading lessons, simple instruction in punctua-
tion and arithmetic, and lists of words of one, two, or three syllables
had been read by the Anglican Rector of Stoke Hammond, Thomas
Disney, and reported to the government authorities as not only unfit
for children, but positively seditious. No copies of this primer exist
today. At the time of his trial all copies of it were destroyed, though
we are told Keach rewrote it later from memory and published it as
The Child's Delight: or Instructions for Children and Youth. The
original primer was deemed heretical especially because of

references to believer's baptism and Keach's interpretation of the Book of Revelation.[8] Put on trial on October 8, 1664, Keach was found guilty, imprisoned for two weeks and fined £20, a considerable amount in those days for a poor Baptist preacher.

In addition to these punishments, Keach had to stand for two periods of two hours each in the pillory, a wooden framework that had holes for the head and hands of the person being punished. Generally the pillory would be placed in the town or village square where the offender could also be subjected to various forms of public ridicule. On this occasion, however, Keach took the opportunity to preach to the crowd that gathered around. "Good people", he began during his first time in the pillory, "I am not ashamed to stand here this day, ... my Lord Jesus was not ashamed to suffer on the cross for me; and it is for his cause that I am made a gazing-stock. Take notice, it is not for any wickedness that I stand here; but for writing and publishing his truths, which the Holy Spirit hath revealed in the Holy Scriptures". At this point a Church of England clergyman, possibly the local minister, sought to silence Keach by telling him that he was in the pillory for "writing and publishing errors". Keach, recognising a golden opportunity for public debate and witness, quickly replied, "Sir, can you prove them errors?" But before the clergyman could respond, he was rounded on by others in the crowd, who knew him to be a drunk. Keach proceeded to speak in defence of his convictions despite a couple of further attempts by the authorities to silence him. Eventually he was told that if he would not be silent, he would have to be gagged. After this he was silent except for his quoting of Matthew 5:10: "Blessed are they which are persecuted for righteousness' sake: for theirs is the kingdom of heaven".[9]

On another occasion, when Keach was apprehended in the act of preaching by a troop of cavalrymen, four of them were so enraged with him that they swore that they would trample him to death with their horses. He was accordingly bound and forced to lie on the ground. But just as they were about to spur their horses down upon their victim, their commanding officer arrived and prevented them from harming Keach, who almost certainly would have been killed.[10]

A move to London and an embrace of Calvinism

In 1668 Keach moved to London, where he joined a General Baptist
cause meeting on Tooley Street in Southwark, London's first suburb
located on the south shore of the Thames river. He was soon
ordained an elder of this congregation. However, not long after his
arrival in London he made the acquaintance of Hanserd Knollys and
William Kiffin, and by the time of his second marriage in 1672 to
Susannah Partridge (d. 1732) of Rickmansworth, Hertfordshire -
Jane, his first wife, had died in 1670 - he had become a Calvinist. Of
the details of this momentous theological move we know nothing.
As the American historian J. Barry Vaughn has noted, the "date and
circumstances of Benjamin Keach's acceptance of Calvinism is the
greatest puzzle of his life".[11] However, the fact that Knollys
officiated at the marriage of Keach to Susannah Partridge certainly
leads one to believe that this influential figure played a rôle in
Keach's coming over to the Calvinistic Baptists. It is interesting to
note that while such a move from the ranks of the General Baptists
to those of the Calvinistic Baptists was not uncommon during the
seventeenth and eighteenth centuries, there was rarely any traffic
the other way.[12]

In the same year of his marriage, Keach and a few like-minded
individuals, possibly former members of the General Baptist cause
on Tooley Street, began a Calvinistic Baptist work in Horsleydown,
Southwark. A meeting house was eventually erected, which, after a
number of additions over the years, could hold up to a thousand or
so people. Keach was evidently a powerful preacher, whose
sermons, his son-in-law later noted, were "full of solid divinity".[13]

In addition to his labours as a pastor, Keach was also active in
planting new works in southern England and regularly employing
his pen to elucidate the Scriptures and defend the Calvinistic Baptist
cause. Of the many subjects upon which he wrote, his contribution
to two in particular would prove to be especially influential. The first
was his defence of a Calvinistic perspective on salvation. During the
1680s and 1690s, at the time when Keach was being widely
published, Calvinism was increasingly a house under attack. The
theology of Puritan theologians like Keach and John Owen was
coming to be regarded with scorn and disdain as outmoded and old-
fashioned. Encouraged by the "middle way" thinking of Richard

Baxter, which sought to develop a theological perspective that toned down some key doctrines of traditional Calvinism and embraced some elements of Arminianism, not a few of the heirs of Puritanism, in particular the English Presbyterians, were involved in a wholesale retreat from their Calvinistic heritage. This was not, however, the case with the Calvinistic Baptists and that in large measure because of the writings of Keach.

Calvinistic views on salvation

Consider, for example, his final major work, *Gospel Mysteries Unveiled*, published only three years before his death in 1704. This work was originally a series of sermons which exhaustively expounded all of Christ's parables and similitudes. The discussion of the parable of the lost sheep (Luke 15:4-7), for instance, ran to sixteen sermons and well over a hundred pages in the four-volume edition that was issued in the 1810s.[14] Now, in his fifteenth sermon on this particular parable, Keach presents an understanding of regeneration and conversion that was common to most Calvinistic Baptists of his day and served to distinguish them from other denominational bodies like the Presbyterians who were fast moving out of the Calvinist orbit.

Keach begins by observing that this parable clearly teaches that "lost sinners cannot go home to God of themselves," but must be carried to him on the shoulders of Christ. To Keach this doctrinal conclusion was clear first of all from the reference to the lost sheep being placed on the shoulders of the shepherd. When other passages of Scripture talk of the "finger of God" (Luke 11:20) or the "arm of the Lord" (Isaiah 53:1), these anthropomorphisms are to be understood as references to God's power. Likewise, Keach reasons, the mention of the shepherd's shoulders in Luke 15:5 must be a reference to "Christ's efficacious and effectual power", especially, given the nature of the parable, as it relates to "regenerating and converting".[15]

Keach then adduces further scriptural proof that regeneration was wholly God's work, a work in which men and women are entirely passive. There was, for example, John 15:5, where Christ informed the apostles, "Without me ye can do nothing". This verse clearly has to do with the living out of the Christian life, but Keach evidently sees principles embedded in it that also apply to entry into that life. Keach understands Christ's statement "without me" to be a reference to Christ's "almighty arm ... made bare" and his "power exerted". If it be true, therefore, that Christ's power is vital for the presence of "acceptable fruit to God" during the Christian life, how much more is it the case that this power is required for "a sinner's implantation into Christ".[16] Yet, because the verse has to do with living a fruitful Christian life, which involves effort on the part of both the believer and Christ, it does not really substantiate Keach's assertion that the sinner is passive in regeneration.

The next verse that he cites, John 6:44a ("No man can come to me, except the Father which hath sent me draw him"), is much more germane. The drawing involved here, according to Keach, is "the sublime and irresistible influences of the holy God upon the heart, by which he inclines, bows, and subjects the stubborn and rebellious will to believe and receive the Lord Jesus Christ". Keach rightly links this verse with one later in the same chapter: "no man can come unto me, except it were given unto him of my Father" (John 6:65). That which is given, Keach emphasises, is what enables a sinner to come to Christ: the gift of the indwelling Spirit, the affections of a new heart, grace, faith and divine power.[17]

The third text that Keach cites is yet another Johannine one, John 1:13. The children of God, this verse asserts, are born " not of blood, nor of the will of the flesh, nor of the will of man, but of God". Regeneration is not based on one's physical lineage, nor on one's "legal privileges" (so Keach reads "nor of the will of the flesh"). Nor is the new birth accomplished by any "power of man's will", for "before a vital principle is infused" into a person, all that he or she can do are "dead works". The "plain and evident" declaration of this verse is that "God is the efficient or great agent in regeneration".[18]

The Baptist preacher then quotes a series of Pauline verses - Romans 9:16; Titus 3:5-6; 2 Corinthians 3:5; 4:7; Philippians 2:12-13 - as further confirmation of his position. With regard to the two texts from 2 Corinthians, Keach especially emphasises that when it came to preaching, it was not the preacher who could effect the change about which he had been talking. It is not "in the power of the most able minister in the world, that the word preached becomes effectual; no, no, ... it is from God" that preaching receives the power to change the hearts of men and women.[19]

In the next section of this sermon Keach provides additional arguments in support of his perspective on regeneration. These are based on a variety of Scripture texts, most of them drawn from the New Testament. It is in this section of the sermon that Keach defines what he understands regeneration and conversion to be. Regeneration he describes as "the forming of Christ in the soul", a new creation or a new birth, which is accomplished by the agency of the Holy Spirit. Keach believes that regeneration takes place when the Holy Spirit comes to indwell a person, and a new nature, that of Christ, is formed within the heart of that individual. By this means the enmity towards God that grips the heart of every unbeliever is taken away, and a love and delight for God as their chiefest good imparted. Moreover, just as an unborn child contributes nothing towards its formation in the womb, so are "sinners wholly passive in regeneration".[20]

When Keach comes to define conversion he includes what he had already said about regeneration and thus appears to blur the distinction between the two terms. Conversion, he states, involves a "two-fold act":

> (1) Passive, which is the act of God's Spirit, by which he infuseth a vital principle, and gracious habits, or divine qualities in the soul: in this act the creature is wholly passive. Christ ... infuses life in the dead soul, as he did to dead Lazarus. (2) Active, whereby through the power of that grace, the sinner being quickened, is capacitated to believe, and return to God: being acted, we act; for the Holy Spirit ... so moves the soul, and the soul acts, and moves towards God. ... first the sinner's heart is turned, and then the sinner returneth, then, and not till then: if Christ sought us not first, and found us not first, and took not us up first by his arms and shoulders of divine power, we should never seek, find, nor return to him.[21]

Although this passage shows Keach failing to observe a clear distinction between the two terms, his meaning is clear. What he calls the "passive" aspect of this "two-fold act" is what he has already termed "regeneration". It is wholly an act of God, to which human beings contribute nothing. The Holy Spirit comes into the soul, and gives it both the power and the desire to turn to God. Thus, it is in regeneration that "the seed of actual conversion is sown" in a person's heart.[22] In conversion, on the other hand, the individual is vitally involved as his or her newly-given capacity to turn to God is now exercised.

Finally, it should be noted that in presenting this solidly Calvinistic perspective on regeneration and conversion Keach was careful to guard against High or Hyper-Calvinism, which, as we have noted in the previous chapter, some of his eighteenth-century heirs would uphold. For example, John Brine (1703-1765), a highly influential theologian among the Calvinistic Baptists in the middle decades of the eighteenth century,[23] was clearly following in Keach's train when he maintained that "regeneration is the infusion of a new principle of spiritual life" into a person, "the production of a principle disposed unto actions holy and well-pleasing unto God, by Jesus Christ". It precedes conversion and is to be considered the latter's "foundation and spring". In regeneration sinners are "merely passive," while in conversion they are most definitely "active".[24]

Yet, one key area in which Brine did not follow Keach had to do with the doctrine of eternal justification, a perspective on justification that had been aired in the middle of the seventeenth century and keenly debated in the 1690s.[25] According to Brine's enunciation of this doctrine, since "God had in his eye, even from everlasting, the atonement made by Christ; and, on the account of Christ's engagement to suffer for the sins of the elect, He acquitted them as really as though Christ had actually suffered the penalty demerited by their transgression", then the elect can be regarded as having been justified from eternity.[26] If this were true, then saving faith is reduced to a realisation of what God has already done in the act of eternal justification. So that style of preaching where the lost are explicitly urged to turn to Christ becomes quite unnecessary. What is needed in preaching is simply the proclamation of what God has done in Christ. God will use that to awaken the elect and show them what he has already done for them.

Keach, however, had steadfastly opposed this position during the 1690s. In his main work on justification, *A Medium betwixt two Extremes* (1698), Keach had pointedly asked: "Do we not all preach to all out of Christ as unto ungodly ones, to such that are under Wrath and Condemnation in their own Persons, and so remain until they believe or have Union with Christ. Our Lord *came not to call the Righteous*, as such, neither self-righteous ones, nor such who in a Gospel-sense are righteous Persons, *but Sinners to repentance*; to such that were really lost in the first *Adam*, and under the Bondage of Sin, and the Law."[27] Men and women become justified only at the point of believing in Christ. Consequently, Keach's pulpit ministry was characterised by vigorous evangelism and regular calls to the unconverted to respond to Christ in faith. According to C. H. Spurgeon, in speaking to the lost Keach was "intensely direct, solemn, and impressive, not flinching to declare the terrors of the Lord, nor veiling the freeness of divine grace".[28] Typical of Keach's evangelistic appeals to the unconverted is the following, cited by Spurgeon to illustrate the above statement:

> Come, venture your souls on Christ's righteousness; Christ is able to save you though you are ever so great sinners. Come to him, throw yourselves at the feet of Jesus. *Look to Jesus*, who came to seek and save them that were lost ... You may have the water of life freely. Do not say, "I want qualifications or a meekness to come to Christ." Sinner, dost thou thirst? Dost thou see a want of righteousness? 'Tis not a righteousness; but 'tis a sense of the want of righteousness, which is rather the qualification thou shouldst look at. Christ hath righteousness sufficient to clothe you, bread of life to feed you, grace to adorn you. Whatever you want, it is to be had in him. We tell you there is help in him, salvation in him. "Through the propitiation in his blood" you must be justified, and that by faith alone.[29]

The hymn-singing controversy

The other key area in which Keach influenced future generations was in the sphere of public worship, in particular, with regard to the singing of hymns.[30] His significance is well summed up in the words of Hugh Martin: Keach was "the first to introduce the regular singing of hymns into the normal worship of an English congregation".[31] While some groups, such as the English Presbyterians and the Congregationalists, were convinced that only the Psalms should be sung in public worship,[32] and others, like the

General Baptists and the Quakers, largely rejected the practice of any form of congregational singing, there were a number of Calvinistic Baptists prior to Keach who believed that their worship should not be songless and that it could include hymns as well as Psalms. The Welsh open communion, open membership Baptist Vavasor Powell (1617-1670) declared his conviction in a personal confession of faith that the "singing of Psalms (particularly Scripture-Psalms), Hymns, and Spiritual songs, is a continued Gospel-ordinance, and duty; and to be performed by all, but especially in the Churches".[33] In 1663 Hanserd Knollys also maintained that the singing of "spiritual Songs and Hymnes" was "an ordinance of God's worship", though, on the basis of 1 Corinthians 14:15, he held that the only legitimate instance of such singing was when the Holy Spirit "dictated" the words and tune. Moreover, it seems that the singing Knollys had in mind was that performed by a solo voice and not congregational.[34] However, in 1680 Hercules Collins published *An Orthodox Catechism* in which there was "an appendix concerning the Ordinance of Singing" that gave clear support for the practice of congregational singing.[35]

Keach had first introduced the singing of a hymn between 1673 and 1675 at the conclusion of the celebration of the Lord's Table in his Southwark congregation. A few years later hymns were also being sung at thanksgiving services. At a church meeting on March 1, 1691, a large majority of the members of the church voted to have a hymn sung following the service every Sunday. Yet, there were some in the church who felt that this practice was an unscriptural innovation. Eventually they left the church in March of 1691 and, after a short sojourn in the church that Hanserd Knollys had pastored for many years, they formed themselves into a new cause that met at Maze Pond. In the articles of faith that the founders of the Maze Pond church drew up in February, 1694, it was explicitly stated that congregational singing was "a gross error equall with common nationall Sett forme Prayer".[36]

The convictions of these dissidents were shared by a number of other leading London Baptists, including William Kiffin, Robert Steed (d. 1700), co-pastor with Hanserd Knollys, and Isaac Marlow (1649-1719), a wealthy jeweller and a prominent member of the Mile End Green Baptist Church. Steed preached against congregational singing on at least one occasion and appears to have encouraged Marlow to publish a book against the practice, which was entitled *A Brief Discourse concerning singing* (1690). Although others would write against congregational singing, it was Marlow who became the chief opponent of the practice. In the course of the hymn-singing controversy, which ran from 1690 to 1698, Marlow wrote no less than eleven books that dealt with the issue.[37] The heat generated by the controversy may be discerned to some degree by the terms that the two sides tossed at each other. Marlow tells us that he was labelled a "Ridiculous Scribbler", "Brasen-Forehead", "Enthusiast", i.e. fanatic, and "Quaker". But Marlow could give as good as he got. He viewed his opponents as "a coterie of book burning papists" who were seeking to undermine the Reformation, for, as far as he was concerned, they were endorsing a practice that had no scriptural warrant at all.[38] These acerbic remarks by both sides in the debate indicate that the division over hymn-singing was no trivial matter. It rent the London Baptist community in two, and, in the words of Murdina MacDonald, "effectively destroyed the capacity of the Calvinistic Baptists as a whole to establish a national organization at this time". As MacDonald further notes, the extent of this division is well revealed by the fact that the community's two elder statesmen, Hanserd Knollys and William Kiffin, found themselves on opposing sides.[39]

Marlow and those who opposed the practice of hymn-singing advanced five main arguments in support of their position.[40] First, they maintained that the use of a pre-composed hymn produces the same effect as the reading of a written prayer, namely formalism, and thus leads to a quenching of the Spirit. They were also convinced that examples of singing in the New Testament era involved the exercise of an "extraordinary" spiritual gift. Since these gifts had ceased with the passing of that era, the examples of singing found in the New Testament could not serve as a precedent for their day. Then they argued that congregational singing compromised the purity of the church, for it might well involve people in the congregation who were not regenerate individuals. Fourth, they believed that public singing in the early church was done by a single voice; it was not a congregational effort at all. Finally, where men and women were involved in congregational singing it was a clear violation of 1 Corinthians 14:34 and 1 Timothy 2:11-12, texts which they understood to mean that women should utter not a word in the public worship of the church.

Though it came early in the controversy, Keach's *The Breach Repaired in God's Worship: or, Singing of Psalms, Hymns, and Spiritual Songs, proved to be an Holy Ordinance of Jesus Christ,* published in 1691, proved to be the definitive answer to these various arguments. Keach was eager to defend the practice of congregational singing because he was convinced that one of the main reasons that Baptist causes of his day were beginning to experience "sad witherings" and a "want of God's Presence, or liveliness of Spirit" was their neglect of this scriptural "ordinance".[41] In other words, far from fostering formalism, the singing of hymns was actually a means of spiritual renewal. The failure to engage in hymn-singing was thus robbing God of "one great part of his glorious Praise" as well as depriving believers of "much sweet and Heavenly Joy and Refreshment".[42]

However, as Alan Clifford has noted, Keach did not build his case primarily upon such pragmatic arguments.[43] He turned to Scripture to demonstrate that the angelic hosts in heaven sing praises to God, as have done the saints of God throughout history. Moreover, Keach was able to cite explicit commands in the New Testament that urge this practice upon believers: Ephesians 5:19, Colossians 3:16, and James 5:13. Responding to the various arguments that were being made against congregational singing, Keach first of all pointed out that if singing in the New Testament was based on an "extraordinary" gift of the Spirit, the same was true of many other areas of the life of the Apostolic Church. "The Apostles had an extraordinary Spirit, nay, an infallible Spirit, in *Preaching*, in *Praying*, in *Prophesying*, in *Interpreting* the Scripture". But, in line with fellow Baptists like Hanserd Knollys (see Chapter 5), Keach was of the opinion that these extraordinary gifts "are all ceased, since none have these miraculous Gifts now". If the logic of those opposed to congregational singing were thus followed, "there's none now can, or ought to *Preach, Pray, Interpret*". If congregational singing is to be rejected because it can only be done on the basis of an "extraordinary" spiritual gift - and since all such gifts have ceased - then the conclusion demanded by the position of Keach's opponents was that "all Ordinances are gone, or must be cast off".[44]

The fear that congregational hymn-singing would involve the unregenerate polluting Baptist assemblies was also decisively answered by Keach. The Baptist divine rightly pointed out that for unbelievers to come into their assemblies and sing with the believers who were present was one thing, believers "joining with Unbelievers, is another". Moreover, if a Christian assembly is not to engage in corporate singing for fear that there might be one or more unbelievers present, can other acts of congregational worship, like prayer, take place? "[In prayer] the Communion together in Spirit is more close and intimate than that of uniting the Voice; so that if it be unlawful to let them sing with us, 'tis unlawful to let them in their Hearts join in Prayer with us. Must not the Children have their Bread, because Strangers will get some of it?" In fact, Keach believed that the reasoning of Marlow and others like him in this regard would ultimately spell an end to evangelism. For was not "Hearing the Word of God preached" just as much a "Sacred Ordinance" as singing? If Marlow's reasoning regarding the latter were applied to the former, then the Baptists should "shut the Doors upon them [i.e. unbelievers]" and worship God by themselves without fear of being polluted![45]

To the argument that "women ought not to sing in the Church, because not suffered to speak in the Church" Keach replied by pointing out that there were certain occasions when it was quite permissible for women to speak in the assembly of God's people. For instance, Keach drew his readers' attention to the fact that when women were admitted into the membership of their local churches they were asked "to give an account of their Conversion in the Church, or how God was pleased to work upon their Souls".[46] In other words, Keach was arguing that 1 Corinthians 14:34 or 1 Timothy 2:11-12 had to be understood as prohibiting women from specific types of speaking in front of the congregation. These texts did not demand from women absolute silence in the meeting house. As such, they could not be used to prohibit women from singing with the male members of the congregation.

Keach's method of replying to the final argument, that singing in the New Testament was a solo affair, was to show simply that singing was "performed with united voices" in the New Testament, as it had been done in the Old Testament era. For instance, the commands to sing in Ephesians 5:19 and Colossians 3:16 are clearly directed "not to any select Christian, but to the whole Church".[47]

Vaughn points that out that in all of this controversy one issue was largely absent, namely, *what* should be sung? Should it be simply Psalms, or can it include hymns of purely human composition? Unlike many English-speaking Protestants of his day, Keach was clearly in favour of singing both. Just as in preaching the preacher is not restricted "to do no more than barely read the Scripture, or quote one Scripture after another, ... but may use other Words to edify the Church, provided they agree with, or are congruous to the Word of Christ", so in singing it was quite permissible to sing hymns composed by men other than the penmen of Scripture as long as the hymns were "absolutely congruous" to God's Word.[48] In arguing like this, Keach is clearly blazing the way for the works of Isaac Watts (1674-1748), the father of the English hymn.

Moreover, like Watts, Keach was not merely content to argue the case for singing hymns, he also wrote them. Keach published two hymnbooks, *Spiritual Melody* (1691) and *Spiritual Songs* (1700), which contained in total over four hundred hymns. Although none of them bear comparison with the finest of Watts' hymns, Keach's compositions are not all to be rejected as mere "doggerel" as they have so often been. There is no doubt that some of his hymns are awful poetry. However, as Vaughn has well shown, Keach was not seeking to be a Christian poet as much as a Christian herald: his hymns were intended to be "metrical doctrine" and "metrical sermons". Sounding forth the great truths of Christianity, they were "long on objective praise and doctrine", though generally "short on inwardness" and Christian experience.[49]

Final days

When Keach was dying in the summer of 1704, he asked Joseph Stennett, one of his fellow Calvinistic Baptist ministers in London, to preach a sermon on a portion of 2 Timothy 1:12 ("I know whom I have believed, and am persuaded that he is able to keep that which I have committed unto him against that day") at his funeral. Stennett readily agreed. As it turned out, though, Stennett was too ill to preach at the time of Keach's death and this sermon on 2 Timothy 1:12 had to be postponed until after the actual funeral. Now, what is fascinating about Keach's request is that he and Stennett differed over which day of the week was to be reserved for Christian worship. Stennett was a convinced Sabbatarian and the church that he pastored met at Pinners' Hall in London for worship on Saturdays. One of a number of Seventh-day Baptist churches that had developed in England since the 1650s, Stennett's congregation thrived under his ministry.[50] In fact, between 1695 and 1700 the Pinners' Hall church received into its membership fifteen individuals who had once been members of Keach's Horsleydown church. And one of these fifteen was Keach's own daughter, Hannah![51]

Quite upset by this loss of members to the Seventh-day congregation, Keach decided to preach a series of sermons against Sabbatarianism, which he subsequently published as *The Jewish Sabbath Abrogated, or The Saturday Sabbatarians Confuted* (1700). Stennett did not reply to this attack on his beliefs, and it appears that Keach's book had no ill effects on their friendship. If it had, Keach would certainly not have asked the Seventh-day Baptist to preach his funeral sermon.

Now, in this small incident from Keach's final days we see the seventeenth-century Calvinistic Baptists at their best: vigorous and firm in their convictions but possessed of a catholic spirit that was conscious of what and what was not essential. Keach's disagreement with Seventh-day convictions was strong enough to impel him to go into print against them. But he was obviously able to recognise that disagreement over this issue was not so vital as to imperil fellowship in the Saviour. Thus, both in terms of character and thought, Keach may be rightly regarded as one of the most significant Calvinistic Baptist divines of the seventeenth century.

Conclusion

With the passing of Keach, a distinct era in Calvinistic Baptist history had come to an end. All of the key leaders who had helped to give shape and substance to this dynamic movement - among whom Kiffin, Knollys and Keach were pre-eminent - had entered into the reward for which they had laboured and longed. Behind them they left a legacy that we have sought to detail in the previous pages and which may be helpfully summarised under three headings.

A confessional heritage

First, these early Baptists were firmly convinced that for their movement to flourish it needed clear doctrinal parameters. Thus, right at the outset of the movement's existence in the 1640s a confession of faith, the *First London Confession of Faith*, was drawn up which clearly indicated where these Baptists stood with regard to the three persons in the Godhead, the authority of Scripture, the person and work of Christ, the way of salvation, the nature of the local church, believer's baptism, and the relationship of church and state. This Confession served the Calvinistic Baptists well for the first few decades of their existence. Then, primarily because of various doctrinal threats, in particular that from the Quakers and that from the defection of Thomas Collier from Reformed truth, a new confession was drafted, the *Second London Confession of Faith*. This Confession would become the standard of Calvinistic Baptist doctrine for many English-speaking Baptists well into the nineteenth century and, in the mercy of God, has been rediscovered by Reformed Baptists in the last few decades. In other words, the seventeenth-century Calvinistic Baptists were not afraid to indicate in detail where they stood doctrinally and, as it were, nail their colours to the mast.

The late eighteenth century, however, would see the beginnings of a movement in Baptist circles away from confessional statements. This movement was rooted in the conviction that the Bible is a sufficient touchstone for doctrine and in the fear that confessions cannot but exercise a tyranny over the conscience. It would gather strength especially in the late nineteenth and early twentieth centuries, and would foster an antipathy among certain groups of Baptists towards confessions of faith that exists down to the present day.[1] But if confessions of faith have the potential to be rivals to Scripture and tyrants of the conscience, how can one explain the position of our seventeenth-century Calvinistic Baptist forebears? As we have seen, they were thoroughly convinced of the pre-eminent authority of Scripture over all merely human traditions and documents and of the fact that "God alone is Lord of the conscience".[2] Yet, they were not at all afraid to make considerable use of confessions that set forth plainly and clearly their convictions as both Christians and Baptists.

The seventeenth-century Calvinistic Baptist position in this regard can only be understood if it is recognised first of all that these Baptist confessions were a way of emphasising the vital importance of orthodox doctrine for the Christian life. Like the Puritan movement out of which they emerged, the Calvinistic Baptists who have been the subject of this book were thoroughly aware of the fact that the coals of orthodoxy are ever necessary for the fire of spirituality.[3] Where orthodox doctrine is regarded as unimportant, the fire of Christian piety will inevitably be quenched. Second, the confessions served as a vehicle of unity, enabling the Calvinistic Baptists to engage vigorously in the task of church-planting as well as providing them with a wall of defence against the inroads of such groups as the Quakers.

Now, to be sure, our times are not those of our Calvinistic Baptist forebears. Yet, their convictions regarding confessions of faith have not ceased to be valid. If Calvinistic and Reformed Baptists today are going to know a vital spirituality, see church growth, and stand against the inroads of erroneous perspectives on the Christian life, a confession of faith is essential.[4]

A congregational heritage

One area in which the seventeenth-century Calvinistic Baptists were not ashamed to declare their beliefs was in the realm of church government and the nature of baptism. As we have shown, they were firmly committed to a congregational form of church government in which the locus of authority, under Christ, was in the hands of the congregation. Building on the Reformation doctrine of the priesthood of all believers and the insights of Robert Browne and other early Separatists, they declared their conviction that the local church is a body of visible saints who willingly agree to walk together under the lordship of Christ. They firmly repudiated the idea of a state church, where the church is more like an army of conscripts than God's free people.

There is little doubt that this concept of the local church gave the early Baptists an intensity in their corporate worship not generally found in the traditional Anglican parish church. For example, Benajmin Keach could maintain that in the public worship of the church the believer can experience "the nearest Resemblance of Heaven" and receive the "clearest manifestations of God's Beauty". More of God's "effectual" and "intimate presence" is known in this context of corporate worship than anywhere else. Citing Psalm 87:2 ("The Lord loveth the gates of Zion more than all the dwellings of Jacob") as proof, the London Baptist unequivocally declared that "the publick Worship of God ought to be preferred before private", though the latter must certainly not be neglected. In sum, the place where "God is most Glorified" is in the midst of a worshipping congregation of visible saints.[5]

It needs to be recognised that this emphasis on congregational authority among the seventeenth-century Baptists did not entail the isolation of the local church. As we have seen, they were equally adamant that there be close coperation between churches sharing the same faith. In the words of David Kingdon, for our Calvinistic Baptist forebears, "inter-church fellowship is no more an option than is church membership for the individual believer in a local church".[6]

Entry into the local church for the seventeenth-century Calvinistic Baptists was by way of believer's baptism.[7] During the seventeenth century the Calvinistic Baptists along with the General

Baptists were the only denominations that insisted upon believer's baptism. They were convinced, however, that they had recovered the New Testament's understanding of baptism as an act done to men or women who were already regenerate. As such, baptism became a public declaration that the person being baptised has been born again and brought out of darkness into God's marvellous light. The fact that baptism was generally performed outdoors in a pond or a lake, a stream or a river made the act an even more forceful declaration. It would not be until well into the nineteenth century that most Baptist churches possessed baptistries built within the precincts of the actual church building.

Baptism as an act of public declaration of one's faith in Christ has been all but lost for many Baptists today because of the practice of the altar call. The latter has become for these Baptists the place of public declaration and baptism reduced to a "mere" step of obedience. The early Calvinistic Baptists, though, knowing nothing of the altar call, had a much richer understanding of baptism - and, in the view of this author, a more biblical perspective on this ordinance.

A Reformed heritage

Although the seventeenth-century Calvinistic Baptists were not backward in confessing their distinctive beliefs, they were also very conscious that they stood in a broader movement that went back to the time of the Reformation, when certain central New Testament truths, especially to do with the doctrine of salvation, had been rediscovered. The Calvinistic Baptists regarded themselves as part of an international Reformed movement that embraced believers throughout Europe.

It was no accident, for example, that the *Second London Confession of Faith* was largely drawn from two other Reformed documents, the *Westminster Confession* and the *Savoy Declaration*. In doing this, the Baptists were explicitly declaring their essential solidarity with other Reformed groups in England and Wales. What united them to these fellow believers was ultimately more significant than those things on which they were divided. One important lesson derived from this particular example is well expressed by Samuel E. Waldron, pastor of the Reformed Baptist

Church in Grand Rapids, Michigan. "How often small, isolated and despised bands of Reformed Baptists or other Reformed Christians have reacted by over-emphasising their distinctives and displaying a vulnerability to all sorts of peculiarities and eccentricities! Such things have destroyed much of their usefulness. What is needed is the same kind of catholicity of spirit manifested by our first fathers. We must, without betraying our convictions, emphasise our oneness of spirit with other conservative and Reformed Christians".[8]

The "catholicity of spirit" of which Waldron speaks here permeates much of seventeenth-century Calvinistic Baptist witness. It is found in Hanserd Knollys' friendship with Henry Jessey despite the latter's refusal to lead his church into the camp of the closed membership, closed communion Baptists. It can be seen in William Kiffin's willingness to allow the closed communion issue not to become a test of fellowship in the Calvinistic Baptist community at the time of that community's general endorsement of the *Second London Confession of Faith* in 1689. It may be glimpsed in Benjamin Keach's invitation to the Seventh-day Baptist Joseph Stennett to preach his funeral sermon in 1704.

It is indeed a rich heritage that the Calvinistic Baptists of the seventeenth century have bequeathed to those in the modern day who share similar convictions. May we and our churches ponder their historical experience well and know, by the grace of God, the joy of living our lives in Christ's "walled sheep-fold and watered garden".

References

Introduction
1 "C. H. Spurgeon's tribute to William Carey", Supplement to the *Baptist Times* (16 April 1992).

Chapter 1
1 Albert W. Wardin, Jr., *Baptist Atlas* (Nashville: Broadman Press, 1980), 5.
2 W. Morgan Patterson, *Baptist Successionism. A Critical View* (Valley Forge: Judson Press, 1969), 19-20. For a more recent rebuttal of successionism, see James Edward McGoldrick, *Baptist Successionism. A Crucial Question in Baptist History* (Metuchen, New Jersey/London: The American Theological Library Association/The Scarecrow Press, Inc., 1994).
3 Patterson, *Baptist Successionism*, 75.
4 William L. Lumpkin, *Baptist Confessions of Faith* (2nd. ed.; Valley Forge: Judson Press, 1969), 285-286.
5 For a good study of this view of Baptist history, see Patterson, *Baptist Successionism* and McGoldrick, *Baptist Successionism.*
6 *Anabaptist Baptism: A Representative Study* (Scottdale, Pennsylvania: Herald Press, 1966), 94.
7 See John Horsch, "Did Menno Simons Practise Baptism by Immersion?" *The Mennonite Quarterly Review*, 1 (1927), 54-56.
8 Kenneth R. Manley, "Origins of the Baptists: The Case For Development from Puritanism-Separatism" in William H. Brackney with Ruby J. Burke, eds., *Faith, Life and Witness. The Papers of the Study and Research Division of The Baptist World Alliance 1986-1990* (Birmingham, Alabama: Samford University Press, 1990), 57.
9 *Ibid.*, 57. See also B. R. White, *The English Baptists of the Seventeenth Century* (London: The Baptist Historical Society, 1983), 22.
10 The *First London Confession of Faith*, Preface (Lumpkin, *Baptist Confessions*, 153).
11 Manley, "Origins of the Baptists", 57. See also White, *English Baptists*, 22. On the Münster episode, see Michael R. Watts, *The Dissenters* (Oxford: Clarendon Press, 1978), 8-9.
12 Manley, "Origins of the Baptists", 57. See also White, *English Baptists*, 22.

13 Cited Manley, "Origins of the Baptists", 57.

14 Robert C. Walton, *The Gathered Community* (London: Carey Press, 1946), 59.

15 B. R. White, *The English Separatist Tradition from the Marian Martyrs to the Pilgrim Fathers* (London: Oxford University Press, 1971), 42. On Browne, see *ibid.*, 44-66; Watts, *Dissenters*, 27-34.

16 White, *English Separatist Tradition*, 45-48.

17 *Ibid.*, 48-49.

18 *Ibid.*, 59.

19 Cited Watts, *Dissenters*, 30.

20 *Ibid.*, 34.

21 *English Separatist Tradition*, 84.

22 Cited Watts, *Dissenters*, 39. For a recent study of Penry, see Geoffrey Thomas, "John Penry and the Marprelate Controversy" in *The Trials of Puritanism. Papers read at the 1993 Westminster Conference* (London: The Westminster Conference, 1993), 45-71.

23 Watts, *Dissenters*, 40.

24 White, *English Separatist Tradition*, 102.

25 B. R. White, "Smyth, John" in Richard L. Greaves and Robert Zaller, eds., *Biographical Dictionary of British Radicals in the Seventeenth Century* (Brighton, Sussex: The Harvester Press, 1984), III, 186; James Robert Coggins, *John Smyth's Congregation: English Separatism, Mennonite Influence, and the Elect Nation* (Waterloo, Ontario/Scottdale, Pennsylvania: Herald Press, 1991), 32. Both of these works have been very helpful in sketching Smyth's career.

26 White, *English Separatist Tradition*, 117-118; Coggins, *John Smyth's Congregation*, 32.

27 For a discussion of these differences, see James R. Coggins, "The Theological Positions of John Smyth", *The Baptist Quarterly*, 30 (1983-1984), 250-252; *idem, John Smyth's Congregation*, 50-55.

28 Coggins, *John Smyth's Congregation*, 56-61.

29 Watts, *Dissenters*, 44.

30 *The Works of John Smyth*, ed. W. T. Whitley (Cambridge: Cambridge University Press, 1915), II, 567-568.

31 *Ibid.*, II, 565, 571. In modernizing this quotation from *The Character of the Beast*, I have followed the modernized version of the introduction to this treatise by Sydnor L. Stealey, comp. and ed., *A Baptist Treasury* (New York: Thomas Y. Crowell Co., 1958), 2-9.

32 See the discussion of Smyth's thinking at this point by White, *English Separatist Tradition*, 137-138.

33 Cited Watts, *Dissenters*, 45.

34 White, *English Separatist Tradition*, 138. Though cf. Coggins, "Theological Positions of John Smyth", 257-258.

35 For the history of the congregation after Smyth's break with Helwys and the former's death, see Coggins, *John Smyth's Congregation*, 107-114.

36 On Helwys, see Ernest A. Payne, *Thomas Helwys and the First Baptist Church in England* (London: The Baptist Union of Great Britain and Ireland, 1959 [?]); B. R. White, "Helwys, Thomas" in Richard L. Greaves and Robert Zaller, eds., *Biographical Dictionary of British Radicals in the Seventeenth Century* (Brighton, Sussex: The Harvester Press, 1983), II, 76-77. On the history of the Helwys congregation after its return to England, see Watts, *Dissenters*, 49-50; Coggins, *John Smyth's Congregation*, 104-107.

Chapter 2

1 "Anabaptist Influence in the Origin of the Particular Baptists", *The Mennonite Quarterly Review*, 36 (1962), 322-323.

2 Cited W. E. Blomfield, "Yorkshire Baptist Churches in the 17th and 18th Centuries" in *The Baptists of Yorkshire* (2nd. ed.; Bradford and London: Wm. Byles & Sons Ltd./London: Kingsgate Press, 1912), 105.

3 Theron D. Price, "The Anabaptist View of the Church" in Duke K. McCall, comp. and ed., *What Is the Church?* (Nashville, Tennessee: Broadman Press, 1958), 112-113.

4 Stassen, "Anabaptist Influence", 325.

5 On Henry Jacob, see especially Stephen Brachlow, "The Elizabethan Roots of Henry Jacob's Churchmanship: Refocusing the Historiographical Lens", *The Journal of Ecclesiastical History*, 36 (1985), 228-254. On the Jacob-Lathrop-Jessey church, see Murray Tolmie, *The Triumph of the Saints. The Separate Churches of London 1616-1649* (Cambridge: Cambridge University Press, 1977), 7-27.

6 Brachlow, "The Elizabethan Roots of Henry Jacob's Churchmanship", 238-239.

7 Paul Linton Gritz, "Samuel Richardson and the Religious and Political Controversies Confronting the London Particular Baptists, 1643 to 1658" (Unpublished Ph. D. thesis, Southwestern Baptist Theological Seminary, 1987), 25-29.

8 On Jessey, see especially B. R. White, "Henry Jessey in the Great Rebellion" in R. Buick Knox, ed., *Reformation Conformity and Dissent. Essays in honour of Geoffrey Nuttall* (London: Epworth Press, 1977), 132-153.

9 This text may be conveniently found in Champlin Burrage, *The Early English Dissenters in the Light of Recent Research (1550-1641)* (Cambridge: Cambridge University Press, 1912), II, 302-305. The text cited is from page 302.

10 On Spilsbury, see R. L. Greaves, "Spilsbury (or Spilsbery), John" in his and Robert Zaller, eds., *Biographical Dictionary of British Radicals in the*

Seventeenth Century (Brighton, Sussex: The Harvester Press, 1984), 193-194; Robert W. Oliver, *From John Spilsbury to Ernest Kevan. The Literary Contribution of London's Oldest Baptist Church* (London: Grace Publications Trust on behalf of the Evangelical Library, 1985), 8-9; B. R. White, "The London Calvinistic Baptist Leadership 1644-1660" in J. H. Y. Briggs, ed., *Faith, Heritage and Witness* (London: The Baptist Historical Society, 1987), 37-38; Gritz, "Samuel Richardson", 26-27.

11 Cited Oliver, *John Spilsbury to Ernest Kevan*, 9.

12 "Henry Jessey", 135.

13 Cited Michael R. Watts, *The Dissenters* (Oxford: Clarendon Press, 1978), 80-81.

14 Burrage, *Early English Dissenters*, II, 302-303.

15 *Ibid.*, II, 303-304.

16 David J. Terry, "Mark Lucar: Particular Baptist Pioneer", *Baptist History and Heritage*, 25, No.1 (January, 1990), 43-49.

17 W. T. Whitley, "The Seven Churches of London", *The Review and Expositor*, 7, No. 3 (July 1910), 387-388.

18 On Kiffin, see below, chapter 5; on Cox, see W. T. Whitley, "Benjamin Cox", *Transactions of the Baptist Historical Society*, 6, No.1 (1918), 50-59.

19 *A Declaration concerning the Publike Dispute concerning Infants-Baptisme* (London: 1645), 4-6.

20 *Ibid.*, 19.

21 *Ibid.*, 14-15.

22 White, "Henry Jessey", 152-153, 143.

Chapter 3

1 Joseph Ivimey, *The Life of Mr. William Kiffin* (London: 1833), 99; B. R. White, "The Doctrine of the Church in the Particular Baptist Confession of 1644", *The Journal of Theological Studies*, N.S., 19 (1968), 570; William L. Lumpkin, *Baptist Confessions of Faith* (2nd. ed.; Valley Forge: Judson Press, 1969), 145-146.

2 The *First London Confession of Faith*, Preface (Lumpkin, *Baptist Confessions*, 154-155).

3 Cited Gordon Kingsley, "Opposition to Early Baptists (1638-1645)", *Baptist History and Heritage*, 4, No.1 (January, 1969), 29. On Daniel Featley, see further W. J. McGlothlin, "Dr. Daniel Featley and the First Calvinistic Baptist Confession", *The Review and Expositor*, 6 (1909), 579-589. For the charge of sexual immorality, see also J. F. McGregor, "The Baptists: Fount of All Heresy" in his and B. Reay, eds., *Radical Religion in the English Revolution* (Oxford: Oxford University Press, 1984), 41-42; James Barry Vaughn, "Public Worship and Practical Theology in the Work of Benjamin Keach (1640-1704)" (Unpublished Ph. D. Thesis, University of St. Andrews, 1989), 60.

4 The *First London Confession of Faith*, Preface (Lumpkin, *Baptist Confessions*, 155).

5 White, "Doctrine of the Church", 571, n.1.

6 Murray Tolmie, *The Triumph of the Saints. The Separate Churches of London 1616-1649* (Cambridge: Cambridge University Press, 1977), 61-65; White, "Doctrine of the Church", 570; *idem*, "The Origins and Convictions of the First Calvinistic Baptists", *Baptist History and Heritage*, 25, No.4 (October, 1990), 45.

7 Robert W. Oliver, "*Baptist Confession* Making 1644 and 1689" (Unpublished paper presented to the Strict Baptist Historical Society, 17 March 1989), 4.

8 Lumpkin, *Baptist Confessions*, 162.

9 *Ibid.*, 163.

10 *Ibid.*, 162.

11 *Ibid.*, 162; Oliver, "Baptist Confession Making", 4.

12 See especially the *First London Confession of Faith* XLVIII-XLIX (Lumpkin, *Baptist Confessions*, 169).

13 See Lumpkin, *Baptist Confessions*, 148.

14 *Ibid.*, 165.

15 White, "Doctrine of the Church", 580.

16 Lumpkin, *Baptist Confessions*, 167. In the second edition of 1646 a clause was added to the end of this article which limited participation in the Lord's Supper to baptised believers.

17 *Ibid.*, 167. For the meaning of baptism in the writings of one of the signatories of this confession, see B. R. White, "Thomas Patient in England and Ireland", *Irish Baptist Historical Society Journal*, 2 (1969-1970), 43-45.

18 Lumpkin, *Baptist Confessions*, 165-166.

19 See, for example, Benjamin Keach, *Gospel Mysteries Unveiled* (London: L. I. Higham, 1815), II, 332: "Some part of a wilderness hath been turned into a garden or fruitful vineyard: so God hath out of the people of this world, taken his churches and walled them about, that none of the wild beasts can hurt them"; *ibid.*, II, 339: "The church of Christ, is a garden inclosed, or a community of Christians distinct from the world: 'A garden inclosed is my sister, my spouse' Cant. iv.12." The covenant of Bourton on the Water Baptist Church, Gloucestershire, drawn up around 1720, stated that members of the church must "promise to keep the Secrets of our Church entire without divulging them to any that are not Members of this particular Body, tho' they may be otherwise dear & near to us; for we believe the Church ought to be as a Garden enclosed & a fountain sealed" [cited Charles W. Deweese, *Baptist Church Covenants* (Nashville, Tennessee: Broadman Press, 1990), 124]. It is noteworthy that Keith W. F. Stavely describes this image of an enclosed garden as "the image most frequently employed to describe the church" in "seventeenth-century

ecclesiastical discourse" ["Roger Williams and the Enclosed Gardens of New England" in Francis J. Bremer, ed., *Puritanism: Transatlantic Perspectives on a Seventeenth-Century Anglo-American Faith* (Boston: Massachusetts Historical Society, 1993), 261].

20 David C. Stuart, *Georgian Gardens* (London: Robert Hale Ltd., 1979), 142-143.

21 Tom Turner, *English Garden Design. History and styles since 1650* (Woodbridge, Suffolk: Antique Collectors' Club Ltd., 1986), 9.

22 Lumpkin, *Baptist Confessions*, 166.

23 *Ibid.*, 168.

24 Michael R. Watts, *The Dissenters* (Oxford: Clarendon Press, 1978), 306-307. It is noteworthy that during the 1640s, according to the Presbyterian controversialist Thomas Edwards (1599-1647), the Calvinistic Baptist leader Hanserd Knollys created "several riots and tumults" by going around churches and speaking after the sermon. See also Rufus M. Jones, *Studies in Mystical Religion* (London: Macmillan, 1909), 424-425.

25 *An Exposition of the whole Book of the Revelation* (London: 1689), 129.

26 The *First London Confession of Faith* XLII (Lumpkin, *Baptist Confessions*, 168).

27 *Ibid.*, 166.

28 White, "Doctrine of the Church", 581; *idem*, "Origins and Convictions of the First Calvinistic Baptists", 46. The first of these articles by White has been very helpful in thinking through the ecclesiology of this Confession. On the fact that there should be only two church offices, those of elder and deacon, see the remarks of Benjamin Keach, *The Glory of a True Church, and its Discipline display'd* (London: 1697), 15-16.

29 "Doctrine of the Church", 584.

30 "A Baptist Ecclesiology for the Contemporary World", *Search*, 22, No.4 (Summer 1993), 8-9.

31 Lumpkin, *Baptist Confessions*, 168-169.

32 White, "Doctrine of the Church", 583-584.

33 R. Dwayne Conner, "Early English Baptist Associations. Their Meaning for Baptist Connectional Life Today", *Foundations*, 15 (1972),167-168, 172-177.

34 "Origins and Convictions of the First Calvinistic Baptists", 47.

Chapter 4

1 *The Life of Mr. William Kiffin* (London: 1833), xi, ii. This work is an annotated and edited version of Kiffin's autobiography.

2 "William Kiffin - Baptist Pioneer and Citizen of London", *Baptist History and Heritage*, 2, No. 2 (July, 1967), 91. Over the years, White has produced a number of sterling pieces on Kiffin's life and states in the above-mentioned article that he was preparing a biography of Kiffin

("William Kiffin", 91, n.1). This biography has yet to appear. Recently, B. A. Ramsbottom has written a popular and extremely readable biography of Kiffin: *Stranger Than Fiction. The Life of William Kiffin* (Harpenden, Hertfordshire: Gospel Standard Trust Publications, 1989). For a review of this book, see Michael A. G. Haykin, "The Life of William Kiffin", *Reformation Today*, 119 (Jan-Feb, 1991), 23-26.

3 W. J. McGlothlin, *Baptist Confessions of Faith* (Philadelphia: American Baptist Publication Society, 1911), 219.

4 White, "William Kiffin", 94. Joseph Ivimey asserts that Kiffin was apprenticed to John Lilburne (*ca.*1615-1657), later one of the leaders of a group of political radicals known as the Levellers [*A History of the English Baptists* (London: 1811), I, 147, 164]. As White points out, this is clearly impossible, since Lilburne was roughly the same age as Kiffin; see his "William Kiffin", 94, n.11.

5 Ivimey, *Life of Mr. William Kiffin*, 2.

6 *Ibid.*, 2-3.

7 Cited White, "William Kiffin", 94.

8 In fact, in the early years of Kiffin's ministry, he appears to have sided with those Puritans who stridently rejected all formal theological training. In 1655, for instance, he wrote a commendatory postscript for Samuel How's *The Sufficiencie of the Spirits Teaching without Humane Learning*, which maintained that human learning is of no help in understanding God's will. How was convinced that of two believers - the one learned, the other not - the latter is to be preferred for vocational ministry, since "the wisdom of this world is foolishness with God". By 1689, though, Kiffin was in favour of recommending that "a competent knowledge of the Hebrew, Greek, and Latin tongues" be obtained by those pastoring Calvinistic Baptist churches, so that these pastors would be better equipped in defending "the truth against opposers" (Ivimey, *History*, I, 500). At the same time, it should be noted, he continued rightly to maintain that, in the final analysis, "the graces and gifts of the Holy Spirit" are "sufficient to the making and continuing of an honourable ministry in the churches" (*ibid.*, I, 499).

9 "To the Christian Reader" in *A Sober Discourse of Right to Church-Communion* (London: 1681).

10 For a more detailed discussion of the way in which Kiffin was led to the Baptist position, see White, "William Kiffin", 95-96; *idem*, "How did William Kiffin join the Baptists?", *The Baptist Quarterly*, 23 (1969-1970), 201-207.

11 "To the Christian Reader".

12 *Stranger Than Fiction*, 18, 102. In a recommendatory preface to *Baptism discovered plainly and faithfully according to the word of God* by John Norcott (1621-1676), William Kiffin said of Norcott: "He steered his

whole course by the compass of the word, making Scripture precept or example his constant rule in matters of religion. Other men's opinions or interpretations were not the standard by which he went; but, through the assistance of the Holy Spirit, he laboured to find out what the Lord himself had said in his word" [cited Joseph Ivimey, *A History of the English Baptists* (London: B. J. Holdsworth, 1823), III, 300]. This statement by Kiffin with regard to Norcott reveals as much about Kiffin's own priorities as it does about Norcott.

13 *First London Confession of Faith* 39 [*The First London Confession of Faith, 1646 Edition* (Repr. Rochester, New York: Backus Book Publishers, 1981), 14].

14 For details of Kiffin's rôle in this regard, see especially White, "William Kiffin", 97.

15 Cited Antonia Fraser, *Cromwell: Our Chief of Men* (1973 ed.; repr. London: Mandarin Paperbacks, 1989), 706.

16 See his speech before Parliament on September 12, 1654 [*Speeches of Oliver Cromwell*, ed. Ivan Roots (London: J.M. Dent & Sons Ltd., 1989), 51-52]. On his tolerance, see especially Geoffrey F. Nuttall, *The Holy Spirit in Puritan Faith and Experience* (2nd. ed.; Oxford: Basil Blackwell, 1947), 126-133; H. F. Lovell Cocks, *The Religious Life of Oliver Cromwell* (London: Independent Press Ltd., 1960), 45-63; Gordon Murray, "Oliver Cromwell - The Father of Toleration?" in *Divisions and Dissensions. Papers read at the 1987 Westminster Conference* ([London]: The Westminster Conference, 1987), 38-56.

17 *The Fourth Paper, Presented by Maior Butler, to the Honourable Committe of Parliament, for the Propagating the Gospel of Christ Jesus* (London: G. Calvert, 1652). Unlike religious toleration in western nations of today, which is largely the result of indifference to religious matters, Cromwell's commitment to such tolerance was rooted in conviction and principle. For a cogent defence of mid-seventeenth-century congregational polity as the major seedbed of later religious toleration, see J. Wayne Baker, "Church, State, and Toleration: John Locke and Calvin's Heirs in England, 1644-1689" in W. Fred Graham, ed., *Later Calvinism: International Perspectives* (Kirksville, Missouri: Sixteenth Century Journal Publishers, Inc., 1994), 525-543.

18 Letter from William Kiffin, John Spilsbury, and Joseph Sansom, 20 January 1654 [in John Nickolls, Jr., ed., *Original Letters and Papers of State Addressed to Oliver Cromwell* (London: 1743), 159-160]. It is noteworthy that Kiffin, in the words of Richard D. Land, was "a strong supporter of Cromwell" ["Doctrinal Controversies of English Particular Baptists (1644-1691) as Illustrated by the Career and Writings of Thomas Collier" (Unpublished D. Phil. Thesis, Oxford University, 1979), 257]. On the relationship of the Calvinistic Baptists to the Fifth Monarchy movement, see especially Louise Fargo Brown, *The Political Activities of*

the Baptists and Fifth Monarchy Men In England During The Interregnum (New York: Burt Franklin, 1911); B. R. White, *The English Baptists of the Seventeenth Century* (London: The Baptist Historical Society, 1983), 84-87, 99-101; Marilyn A. Hartman, "For Christ and the People": The Ideology of the Good Old Cause, 1653-1660" (Unpublished Ph.D. thesis, Indiana University, 1977), 82-91. The words "harmless Bible students" are those of White (*English Baptists*, 85).

19 For further discussion of this event, see White, "William Kiffin", 97-98.

20 *Ibid.*, 126.

21 *Ibid.*, 91.

22 For an account of this story, see Ivimey, *History*, I, 336-338.

23 *The History of the English Baptists* (London: 1740), III, 4.

24 Ivimey, *Life*, 63.

25 *Ibid.*, 64. For the full account of the trial of the Hewlings and the Christian manner in which they conducted themselves at the time of their respective deaths, see *ibid.*, 62-84. White describes Jefferies as "the unspeakable Judge Jefferies" ("William Kiffin", 102).

26 William is often portrayed by historians as a committed Calvinist. However, in a recent study of William's religious commitment, Jonathan I. Israel has argued that William's personal religiosity was "decidedly tepid," despite the fact that as a young boy he had been under the tutelage of Cornelius Trigland, a pillar of Dutch Calvinism ["William III and Toleration" in Ole Peter Grell, Jonathan I. Israel, and Nicholas Tyacke, eds., *From Persecution to Toleration. The Glorious Revolution and Religion in England* (Oxford: Clarendon Press, 1991), 129-170].

27 Cited Ivimey, *History*, III, 336.

28 *Second London Confession of Faith*, (McGlothlin, *Baptist Confessions*, 287).

29 Robert W. Oliver, "Baptist Confession Making 1644 and 1689" (Unpublished paper presented to the Strict Baptist Historical Society, 17 March, 1989), 17.

30 T. E. Dowley, "A London Congregation during the Great Persecution: Petty France Particular Baptist Church, 1641-1688", *The Baptist Quarterly*, 27 (1977-1978), 233-234.

31 Oliver, "Baptist Confession Making", 20.

32 Quoted Ivimey, *History*, I, 490.

33 A. C. Underwood, *A History of the English Baptists* (London: The Baptist Union Publication Dept. (Kingsgate Press), 1947), 129; Joshua Thompson, "The Communion Controversy and Irish Baptists", *Irish Baptist Historical Society Journal*, 20 (1987-1988), 29-30.

34 "Open and Closed Membership among English and Welsh Baptists", *The Baptist Quarterly*, 24 (1971-1972), 332; *idem*, *English Baptists*, 9.

35 *The Records of a Church of Christ in Bristol, 1640-1687*, ed. Roger Hayden (Bristol: Bristol Record Society, 1974), 52-53. Kiffin's relation-

ship with the Broadmead Church appears to have been cordial; see White, *English Baptists*, 112.

36 On the controverted question about whether or not Bunyan actually was a Baptist, see Thomas Armitage, *A History of the Baptists* (New York: Bryan, Taylor, & Co., 1887), 529-539; John Brown, *John Bunyan (1628-1688): His Life, Times, and Work*, revised Frank Mott Harrison (London/ Glasgow/Birmingham: The Hulbert Publishing Co., 1928), 221-225, 236-238; Joseph D. Ban, "Was John Bunyan a Baptist? A Case-Study in Historiography", *The Baptist Quarterly*, 30 (1983-1984), 367-376. This author would agree with the estimation of Richard L. Greaves when he states that "Bunyan is rightly regarded as an open membership Baptist" ["Conscience, Liberty, and the Spirit: Bunyan and Nonconformity" in N. H. Keeble, ed., *John Bunyan: Conventicle and Parnassus. Tercentenary Essays* (Oxford: Clarendon Press, 1988), 35]. In this regard, see also Kenneth Dix, *John Bunyan: Puritan Pastor* ([Dunstable, Bedfordshire]: The Fauconberg Press for The Strict Baptist Historical Society, 1978), 8.
37 *Sober Discourse*, 16-17. The description of this treatise is taken from T. L. Underwood, " "It pleased me much to contend": John Bunyan as Controversialist", *Church History*, 57 (1988), 468.
38 "William Kiffin", 103.
39 Ivimey, *Life*, 57.
40 *Ibid.*, 58.
41 Murdina D. MacDonald, "London Calvinistic Baptists 1689-1727: tensions within a Dissenting community under Toleration" (Unpublished D. Phil. Thesis, Oxford University, 1982), 181.
42 Ivimey, *Life*, 94-95.

Chapter 5

1 For two recent studies of Knollys' life and ministry, see Pope A. Duncan, *Hanserd Knollys: Seventeenth-Century Baptist* (Nashville, Tennessee: Broadman Press, 1965) and B. R. White, *Hanserd Knollys and Radical Dissent In the 17th Century* (London: Dr. Williams's Trust, 1977). For a helpful biographical sketch, see B. R. White, "Knollys, Hanserd (c.1599-1691)" in Richard L. Greaves and Robert Zaller, eds., *Biographical Dictionary of British Radicals in the Seventeenth Century* (Brighton, Sussex: Harvester Press, 1983), 2:160-162.
2 *The Life and Death of that Old Disciple of Jesus Christ, and Eminent Minister of the Gospel, Mr. Hanserd Knollys* (London: E. Huntington, 1812), 11.
3 *Ibid.*, 12.
4 *Ibid.*, 17.
5 *Ibid.*, 32-33. See also Hanserd Knollys, *Christ Exalted: A Lost Sinner Sought, and saved by Christ: God's people are an Holy people* (London: 1646), i.

6 Murray Tolmie, *The Triumph of the Saints: The Separate Churches of London 1616-1649* (Cambridge: Cambridge University Press, 1977), 60.

7 Michael R. Watts, *The Dissenters* (Oxford: Clarendon Press, 1978), 160.

8 J. F. McGregor, "Seekers and Ranters" in his and B. Reay, eds., *Radical Religion in the English Revolution* (Oxford: Oxford University Press, 1984), 122-123. On the origins of the Seekers, see Watts, *Dissenters*, 185-186. Many of the Seekers eventually became Quakers (*ibid.*, 193, 195-196, 204). In the words of Tolmie, *Triumph of the Saints*, 6: "The Quakers succeeded in giving shape and direction to the spiritual turmoil of Seekers and anti-formalists."

9 In outlining Erbery's thought, the following have been very helpful: Christopher Hill, *The Experience of Defeat. Milton and Some Contemporaries* (London: Faber and Faber, 1984), 84-97; B. R. White, "William Erbery (1604-1654) and the Baptists", *The Baptist Quarterly*, 23 (1969-1970), 114-125. Erbery's works were collected together after his death and published as *The Testimony of William Erbery, Left Upon Record for The Saints of succeeding Ages* (London: Giles Calvert, 1658).

10 *The Children of the West. Or, The Fears of all who are in Forms, especially of Water-Baptism* (*Testimony*, 138).

11 *The great Earthquake, Revel. 16.18* (*Testimony*, 302).

12 *Children of the West* (*Testimony*, 136, 137).

13 On Saltmarsh's life and thought, see Leo F. Solt, "John Saltmarsh: New Model Army Chaplain", *The Journal of Ecclesiastical History*, 2 (1951), 69-80; N. T. Burns, "Saltmarsh, John (c.1612-1647)" in Richard L. Greaves and Robert Zaller, eds., *Biographical Dictionary of British Radicals in the Seventeenth Century* (Brighton, Sussex: Harvester Press, 1984), 3:136-137. Knollys' response to Saltmarsh was one of a number of Baptist works written against the Seekers. See Tolmie, *Triumph of the Saints*, 54-55.

14 *The Smoke in the Temple* (London: G. Calvert, 1646), 17-18.

15 *The Shining of a Flaming Fire in Zion* (London: 1646), 9.

16 *Ibid.*, 9.

17 See W. P. Stephens, *The Holy Spirit in the Theology of Martin Bucer* (Cambridge: Cambridge University Press, 1970), 185-189; Leonard Sweetman, Jr., "The Gifts of the Spirit: A Study of Calvin's Comments on 1 Corinthians 12:8-10, 28; Romans 12:6-8; Ephesians 4:11" in David E. Holwerda, ed., *Exploring the Heritage of John Calvin* (Grand Rapids: Baker Book House, 1976), 273-303.

18 *Shining of a Flaming Fire*, 10.

19 Cited Victor Budgen, *The Charismatics and the Word of God* (Welwyn, Hertfordshire: Evangelical Press, 1985), 144.

20 *Shining of a Flaming Fire*, 15.

21 *The Gospel Minister's Maintenance Vindicated* (London: 1689), 7.

22 *Christ Exalted*, 11, 4.

23 *Ibid.*, 10.
24 *Ibid.*, 7.
25 *Ibid.*, 11.
26 Knollys' name was variously spelt. See Duncan, Hanserd Knollys, 9, no.3.
27 *The History of the English Baptists* (London: 1740), IV, 307-308. For a couple of other similar incidents from Knollys' life, see Michael A. G. Haykin, "Hanserd Knollys (ca. 1599-1691) on the Gifts of the Spirit", *The Westminster Theological Journal*, 54 (1992), 110-112.
28 Joseph Ivimey, *A History of the English Baptists* (London: 1814), II, 23.
29 *The Works of John Owen* (ed. William H. Goold; 1850-1853 ed.; repr. Edinburgh: Banner of Truth 1967, IV, 475). For discussions of the approach of the Puritans to the extraordinary gifts of the Spirit, see J. I. Packer, "The Puritans and Spiritual Gifts" in *Profitable for Doctrine and Reproof* (London: The Puritan Conference, 1967), 15-27; Garth B. Wilson, "The Puritan Doctrine of the Holy Spirit: A Critical Investigation of a Crucial Chapter in the History of Protestant Theology" (Unpublished Th.D. Thesis, Knox College, Toronto, 1978), 292-300; Budgen, *Charismatics*, 133-145; Sinclair B. Ferguson, *John Owen on the Christian Life* (Edinburgh: Banner of Truth, 1987), 201-208.
30 *Life and Death of Hanserd Knollys*, 58-67.
31 *The Baptist Magazine*, 5 (1813), 78.

Chapter 6
1 See Michael R. Watts, *The Dissenters* (Oxford: Clarendon Press, 1978), 221-222.
2 *Ibid.*, 222.
3 *Ibid.*, 222.
4 Cited T. E. Dowley, "A London Congregation during the Great Persecution: Petty France Particular Baptist Church, 1641-1688", *The Baptist Quarterly*, 27 (1977-1978), 233.
5 While most of the articles in the *Savoy Declaration* are taken word for word from the *Westminster Confession*, there are a number where the authors of the *Savoy Declaration* have either altered the wording or added brand new articles. For some of these changes, see Peter Toon, *Puritans and Calvinism* (Swengel, Pennsylvania: Reiner Publications, 1973), 77-84; Robert W. Oliver, "Baptist Confession Making 1644 and 1689" (Unpublished paper presented to the Strict Baptist Historical Society, 17 March 1989), 11-12.
6 *Second London Confession of Faith*, Preface [William L. Lumpkin, *Baptist Confessions of Faith* (Rev. ed.; Valley Forge: Judson Press, 1969), 244-245].
7 Cited Joseph Ivimey, *A History of the English Baptists* (London: 1811), I, 416.

8 Cited *ibid.*, I, 417-418.

9 Oliver, "Baptist Confession Making", 12-13.

10 Cited Barry Reay, *The Quakers and the English Revolution* (New York: St. Martin's Press, 1985), 33. For a discussion of Fisher's approach to Scripture, see Dean Freiday, *The Bible: Its Criticism, Interpretation and Use in 16th and 17th Century England* (Pittsburgh: Catholic and Quaker Studies, 1979), 97-102.

11 Cited Geoffrey F. Nuttall, *The Holy Spirit in Puritan Faith and Experience* (2nd. ed.; Oxford: Basil Blackwell, 1947), 32.

12 Cited Reay, *Quakers*, 34.

13 For an excellent study of this phenomenon, see Kenneth L. Carroll, "Early Quakers and "Going Naked as a Sign"", *Quaker History*, 67 (1978), 69-87. The following paragraph is indebted to this study. See also Richard Bauman, *Let Your Words Be Few: Symbolism of Speaking and Silence among Seventeenth-Century Quakers* (Cambridge: Cambridge University Press, 1983), 84-94.

14 "Penington, Isaac (the Younger)" in Richard L. Greaves and Robert Zaller, eds., *Biographical Dictionary of British Radicals in the Seventeenth Century* (Brighton, Sussex: The Harvester Press, 1984), III, 23.

15 *Letters of Isaac Penington* (2nd. ed.; repr. London: Holdsworth and Ball, 1829), 202-203. For access to these letters I am indebted to Heinz G. Dschankilic.

16 See also the remarks by Richard Dale Land, "Doctrinal Controversies of English Particular Baptists (1644-1691) as Illustrated by the Career and Writings of Thomas Collier" (Unpublished D. Phil. Thesis, Regent's Park College, Oxford University, 1979), 205-211. In the words of Richard Bauman (*Let Your Words Be Few*, 38): "The Quakers were intensely devoted to the Bible, not as a source of traditional authority, but as historical validation of the patterns and dynamics of their own charismatic prophetic mission".

17 B. R. White, "The Frontiers of Fellowship Between English Baptists, 1609-1660", *Foundations*, 11 (1968), 250.

18 Dowley, "London Congregation", 237; Land, "Doctrinal Controversies", 191-192.

19 Oliver, "Baptist Confession Making", 13. For a full examination of Collier's ministry and writings, see Land, "Doctrinal Controversies".

20 Cited Thompson Cooper, "Collier, Thomas", *The Dictionary of National Biography* (1887 ed.; repr. Oxford: Oxford University Press, 1963-1964), IV, 810-811.

21 Oliver, "Baptist Confession Making", 13.

22 For biographical details of Nehemiah Coxe, see Dowley, "London Congregation", 238, n.12; Joseph Ivimey, *A History of the English Baptists* (London: 1814), II, 403-407.

23 On William Collins, see Ivimey, *History*, II, 397-403.

24 Christopher Hill, *A Turbulent, Seditious, and Factious People: John Bunyan and his Church, 1628-1688* (Oxford: Clarendon Press, 1988), 122.
25 Lumpkin, *Baptist Confessions*, 245.
26 *Westminster Confession* 3.3; *Savoy Declaration* 3.3; *Second London Confession* 3.3 (Lumpkin, *Baptist Confessions*, 254).
27 *Westminster Confession* 21.5; *Savoy Declaration* 22.5; *Second London Confession* 22.5 (Lumpkin, *Baptist Confessions*, 281). For further discussion of this issue, see Chapter 8.
28 "Baptist Confession Making", 21.
29 Cited Lumpkin, *Baptist Confessions*, 239.

Chapter 7

1 *Baptists and the Bible. The Baptist doctrines of biblical inspiration and religious authority in historical perspective* (Chicago: Moody Press, 1980), 62.
2 *Second London Confession* 1.1 (Lumpkin, *Baptist Confessions*, 248). The following analysis of this sentence is indebted to Bush and Nettles, *Baptists and the Bible*, 65-72.
3 *Second London Confession* 1.6 (Lumpkin, *Baptist Confessions*, 250).
4 *Second London Confession* 1.1 (*ibid.*, 248).
5 *Second London Confession* 1.6 (*ibid.*, 250).
6 *Baptists and the Bible*, 68.
7 *Ibid.*, 70. For this definition of the terms "inerrant" and "infallible", see J. I. Packer, "Infallibility and Inerrancy of the Bible" in Sinclair B. Ferguson, David F. Wright, and J. I. Packer, eds., *New Dictionary of Theology* (Downers Grove, Illinois: Inter-Varsity Press, 1988), 337. See also *idem, 'Fundamentalism' and the Word of God. Some Evangelical Principles* (London: Inter-Varsity Fellowship, 1958), 94-96.
8 Richard Dale Land, "Doctrinal Controversies of English Particular Baptists (1644-1691) as Illustrated by the Career and Writings of Thomas Collier" (Unpublished D. Phil. Thesis, Regent's Park College, Oxford University, 1979), 205.
9 *TROPOLOGIA: A Key to Open Scripture-Metaphors* (London: Enoch Prosser, 1681), II, 312.
10 *Second London Confession* 1.5 (Lumpkin, *Baptist Confessions*, 250). For the importance of balance in this area, see the remarks of D. Martyn Lloyd-Jones, *Authority* (1958 ed.; repr. Edinburgh: The Banner of Truth Trust, 1984), 62-64.
11 "John Calvin the Theologian" in his *Calvin as a Theologian and Calvinism Today* (London: Sovereign Grace Union, [1951]), 9.
12 Benjamin B. Warfield, "Introductory Note" to Abraham Kuyper, *The Work of the Holy Spirit*, trans. Henri De Vries (1900 ed.; repr. Grand Rapids: Wm. B. Eerdmans Publishing Co., 1956), xxxiii, xxxv.
13 Of the forty-five or so explicit references to the Holy Spirit in the

Confession, the majority focus on the Spirit's rôle in applying God's saving work to believers. See the remarks of Douglas J. W. Milne regarding the pneumatology of the *Westminster Confession*: "The Doctrine of the Holy Spirit in the Westminster Confession", *The Reformed Theological Review*, 52 (1993), 121.

14 Lumpkin, *Baptist Confessions*, 264-265.

15 For a discussion of this article from somewhat differing positions, see Peter Toon, *Puritans and Calvinism* (Swengel, Pennsylvania: Reiner Publications, 1973), 80-83; Alan P. F. Sell, *The Great Debate, Calvinism, Arminianism and Salvation* (1982 ed.; repr. Grand Rapids: Baker Book House, 1983), 39-40.

16 *Second London Confession* 20.4 (Lumpkin, *Baptist Confessions*, 278-279).

17 *Second London Confession* 7.2 (*ibid.*, 259-260).

18 *Second London Confession* 14.1 (*ibid.*, 268).

19 *Second London Confession* 10.1; 14.1 (*ibid.*, 264, 268). See also Milne, "Doctrine of the Holy Spirit", 126.

20 *Second London Confession* 13.1, 2-3 (Lumpkin, *Baptist Confessions*, 267-268). For other references to the Holy Spirit as a sanctifying Spirit, see, for instance, *Second London Confession* 15.3; 16.3; 17.1 (*ibid.*, 270, 271, 272-273). See also the remarks of Milne, "Doctrine of the Holy Spirit", 127.

21 *Of the Mortification of Sin in Believers* [*The Works of John Owen*, ed. William H. Goold (1850-1853 ed.; repr. Edinburgh: The Banner of Truth Trust, 1965), VI, 16].

22 Cited J. I. Packer, "The Puritan Treatment of Justification by Faith", *The Evangelical Quarterly*, 24 (1952), 143.

23 For the way in which this particular sentence is phrased, I am indebted to George Verwer, *Revolution of Love and Balance* Rev. ed.; Bromley, Kent/Waynesboro, Georgia: STL Books, 1980), 19.

24 Lumpkin, *Baptist Confessions*, 272-273. See also Milne, "Doctrine of the Holy Spirit", 128.

25 Lumpkin, *Baptist Confessions*, 295.

26 *Ibid.*, 259.

27 Robert William Oliver, "The Emergence of a Strict and Particular Baptist Community Among the English Calvinistic Baptists, 1770-1850" (Unpublished Ph.D. Thesis, London Bible College, 1986), 16.

28 *Christ Exalted: A Lost Sinner Sought, and Saved by Christ* (London: 1646), 12.

29 *Key to Open Scripture-Metaphors*, II, 313, 140.

30 "Strict and Particular Baptist Community", 20-21.

31 *Second London Confession* 30.2-6 (Lumpkin, *Baptist Confessions*, 291-293).

32 *Second London Confession* 30.7 (*ibid.*, 293).

33 It should be noted that both the *Westminster Confession* and the *Savoy Declaration* do use the term "ordinance" in later paragraphs to describe the Lord's Supper.

34 W. Morgan Patterson, "The Lord's Supper in Baptist History", *Review and Expositor*, 66, No.1 (Winter, 1969), 26. Cf., however, Erroll Hulse's discussion of these two terms in "The Implications of Baptism" in his *et al. Local Church Practice* (Haywards Heath, Sussex: Carey Publications, 1978), 46-47.

35 *Westminster Confession of Faith* 29.7 [*The Confession of Faith of the Assembly of Divines at Westminster*, ed. S. W. Carruthers (Glasgow: Free Presbyterian Publications, 1978), 22-23]; *Savoy Declaration* 30.7 [*The Savoy Declaration of Faith and Order 1658* (London: Evangelical Press, 1971), 41]. There is one slight difference between the *Westminster Confession* and the *Savoy Declaration*. Where the former reads "in, with, or under the bread *and* wine," the latter has "in, with, or under the bread *or* wine" [italics added].

36 *Second London Confession* 30.7 (Lumpkin, *Baptist Confessions*, 293).

37 For the Puritan rejection of Luther's position, see John F. H. New, *Anglican and Puritan. The Basis of Their Opposition, 1558-1640* (Stanford, California: Stanford University Press, 1964), 60.

38 Cited Ernest F. Kevan, *London's Oldest Baptist Church, Wapping 1633-Walthamstow 1933* (London: The Kingsgate Press, [1933]), 68. On Collins and his ministry, see *ibid.*, 38-50, 64-68.

39 Cited E. P. Winter, "Calvinist and Zwinglian Views of the Lord's Supper Among the Baptists of the Seventeenth Century", *The Baptist Quarterly*, 15 (1953-1954), 327.

40 *A Sober Discourse of Right to Church-Communion* (London: 1681), 25.

41 "The Lord's Supper in the Theology and Practice of Calvin" in G. E. Duffield, ed., *John Calvin* (Grand Rapids: Wm. B. Eerdmans Publishing Co., 1966), 133-134. Another good discussion of Calvin's treatment of the Lord's Supper is John D. Nicholls, "'Union with Christ': John Calvin on the Lord's Supper" in *Union and Communion, 1529-1979* (London: The Westminster Conference, 1979), 35-54.

42 Lumpkin, *Baptist Confessions*, 291.

43 *Key to Open Scripture-Metaphors*, II, 312.

44 For the Puritan view of the Lord's Table, see Geoffrey F. Nuttall, *The Holy Spirit in Puritan Faith and Experience* (2nd. ed.; Oxford: Basil Blackwell, 1947), 90-101; New, *Anglican and Puritan*, 59-76; Hywel W. Roberts, " 'The Cup of Blessing': Puritan and Separatist Sacramental Discourses" in *Union and Communion*, 55-71.

45 See Derek R. Moore-Crispin, " 'The Real Absence': Ulrich Zwingli's View of the Lord's Supper" in *Union and Communion*, 22-34.

46 See, for instance, the comments in the "Introduction" to *A Faith to*

Confess. The Baptist Confession of Faith of 1689 (4th. ed.; Haywards Heath, Sussex: Carey Publications Ltd., 1982), 10-13.

47 Cited in the "Foreword" to *The Baptist Confession of Faith with Scripture Proofs* (Choteau, Montana: Gospel Mission, n.d.), 6. For further comment on the current usefulness of the *Second London Confession*, see Erroll Hulse, "The Reformed Confessions of 17th Century England", *The Evangelical Library Bulletin*, 83 (August 1989), 7; *idem*, "The 1689, Why Another Confession?" (Unpublished paper), 17-19.

Chapter 8

1 "Radical Sects and Dissenting Churches, 1600-1750" in Sheridan Gilley and W. J. Sheils, eds., *A History of Religion in Britain. Practice and Belief from Pre-Roman Times to the Present* (Oxford/Cambridge, Massachusetts: Basil Blackwell Ltd., 1994), 205.

2 "London Calvinistic Baptists 1689-1727: Tensions Within a Dissenting Community under Toleration" (Unpublished D. Phil. Thesis, Regent's Park College, University of Oxford, 1982), 77. On Collins, see Robert W. Oliver, *From John Spilsbury to Ernest Kevan. The Literary Contribution of London's Oldest Baptist Church* (London: Grace Publications Trust on behalf of the Evangelical Library, 1985), 9-11; on Stennett, see B. A. Ramsbottom, *Through Cloud and Sunshine. Four generations of faithful witness - he story of the Stennett family* (N. p.: Gospel Standard Trust Publications, 1982), 4-7.

3 Keach believed that the laying on of hands was an ordinance of "deeply experimental significance" and that those who submit to it receive a "further increase" of the Spirit of God [J. K. Parratt, "An Early Baptist on the Laying on of Hands", *The Baptist Quarterly*, 21 (1966-1967), 325-327, 320].

4 James Barry Vaughn, "Benjamin Keach" in Timothy George and David S. Dockery, eds., *Baptist Theologians* (Nashville, Tennessee: Broadman Press, 1990), 68.

5 The major source of information about Keach comes from his son-in-law, the early Baptist historian Thomas Crosby. See his *The History of the English Baptists* (London: 1740), IV, 268-314. For more recent accounts of his life, see Hugh Martin, *Benjamin Keach (1640-1704): Pioneer of Congregational Hymn Singing* (London: Independent Press Ltd., 1961); James Barry Vaughn, "Public Worship and Practical Theology in the Work of Benjamin Keach (1640-1704)" (Unpublished Ph. D. Thesis, University of St. Andrews, 1989), 6-28; *idem*, "Benjamin Keach" in George and Dockery, eds., *Baptist Theologians*, 49-76. For a brief sketch of his life, see R. L. Greaves, "Keach (or Keeche), Benjamin" in his and Robert Zaller, eds., *Biographical Dictionary of British Radicals in the Seventeenth Century* (Brighton, Sussex: The Harvester Press, 1983), II, 150-151.

6 On the history of this meeting house, see Kenneth Dix, *Benjamin Keach and a monument to liberty* (Dunstable, Bedfordshire: The Fauconberg Press, 1985).

7 Cited Martin, *Benjamin Keach*, 3.

8 On Keach's eschatology, see Kenneth G. C. Newport, "Benjamin Keach, William of Orange and the Book of Revelation: A Study in English Prophetical Exegesis", *The Baptist Quarterly,* 36 (1995-1996), 43-51.

9 Crosby, *History,* II, 204-208.

10 *Ibid.*, II, 185-186.

11 "Public Worship and Practical Theology", 18. For a discussion of possible circumstances, see *ibid.*, 18-22.

12 B. R. White, *The English Baptists of the Seventeenth Century* (London: The Baptist Historical Society, 1983), 7-8.

13 Crosby, *History*, IV, 305.

14 *Gospel Mysteries Unveiled: or, An Exposition of All the Parables and Many Similitudes spoken by Our Lord and Saviour Jesus Christ* (London: L. I. Higham, 1815), II, 321-428. On the composition of *Gospel Mysteries Unveiled* and its style, see Vaughn, "Public Worship and Practical Theology", 89-127.

15 *Gospel Mysteries Unveiled*, II, 392-393.

16 *Ibid.*, II, 394.

17 *Ibid.*, II, 394-395.

18 *Ibid.*, II, 395-396.

19 *Ibid.*, II, 396-397.

20 *Ibid.*, II, 400-401, 404-405, 407-408, 412.

21 *Ibid.*, II, 405-406.

22 *Ibid.*, II, 406.

23 On Brine, see Walter Wilson, *The History and Antiquities of Dissenting Churches and Meeting Houses in London, Westminster, and Southwark* (London: 1808), II, 574-579; Peter Toon, *The Emergence of Hyper-Calvinism in English Nonconformity 1689-1765* (London: The Olive Tree, 1967), 100-102.

24 *A Treatise on Various Subjects*, revised J. A. Jones (4th. ed.; London: James Paul, 1851), 48, 52; *Some Mistakes in a Book of Mr. Johnson's of Liverpool, Intitled, The Faith of God's Elect* (London: John Ward, 1755), 33.

25 For a discussion of this doctrine, see R. T. Kendall, *Calvin and English Calvinism to 1649* (Oxford: Oxford University Press, 1979), 186-187; Robert William Oliver, "The Emergence of a Strict and Particular Baptist Community among the English Calvinistic Baptists 1770-1850" (Unpublished Ph. D. Thesis, London Bible College, 1986), 23-24; Peter Naylor, *Picking Up a Pin for the Lord: English Particular Baptists from 1688 to the Early Nineteenth Century* (London: Grace Publications Trust, 1992), 173-185.

26 *A Defence of the Doctrine of Eternal Justification* (1732 ed.; repr. Paris, Arkansas: The Baptist Standard Bearer, Inc., 1987), 41.

27 *A Medium betwixt two Extremes* (London: Andrew Bell, 1698), 31. On Keach's perspective on justification, see further Vaughn, "Public Worship and Practical Theology", 208-242, *passim*.

28 *The Metropolitan Tabernacle; Its History and Work* (London: Passmore and Alabaster, 1876), 31.

29 Cited *ibid.*, 31.

30 There is a significant amount of literature on Keach's place in the history of English hymnody. See especially Hugh Martin, "The Baptist Contribution to Early English Hymnody", *The Baptist Quarterly*, 19 (1961-1962), 195-208; David W. Music, "The Hymns of Benjamin Keach: An Introductory Study", *The Hymn*, (July 1983), 147-154; James Patrick Carnes, "The Famous Mr. Keach: Benjamin Keach and His Influence on Congregational Singing in Seventeenth Century England" (Unpublished M. A. Thesis, North Texas State University, 1984); Alan Clifford, "Benjamin Keach and Nonconformist Hymnology" in *Spiritual Worship* (London: Westminster Conference, 1985), 69-93; Vaughn, "Public Worship and Practical Theology", 128-187; Donald C. Brown, "To Sing or Not to Sing: Seventeenth Century English Baptists and Congregational Song" in *Handbook to The Baptist Hymnal* (Nashville, Tennessee: Convention Press, 1992), 55-64. On the hymn-singing controversy among the Calvinistic Baptists, see especially MacDonald, "London Calvinistic Baptists", 49-82, *passim*.

31 "Baptist Contribution", 199.

32 See, in this regard, the *Westminster Confession of Faith* 21.5 and the *Savoy Declaration* 22.5.

33 *The Life and Death of Mr. Vavasor Powell, that Faithful Minister and Confessor of Jesus Christ* (N. p.: 1671), 41.

34 Hanserd Knollys, "[To the] Courteous Reader", preface to Katherine Sutton, *A Christian Woman's Experiences of the glorious working of God's free grace* (Rotterdam: Henry Goddaeus, 1663). It is noteworthy that by the time of the hymn-singing controversy Knollys had come to believe in the legitimacy of the congregational singing of hymns.

35 Carnes, "Famous Mr. Keach", 82. For a brief summary of Collins' views in this regard, which are very close to those of Keach, see MacDonald, "London Calvinistic Baptists", 165-166.

36 MacDonald, "London Calvinistic Baptists", 88. For the early development of the Maze Pond cause, see *ibid.*, 83-108.

37 For a list, see *ibid.*, 387-391.

38 *Ibid.*, 62, 72-73, 74.

39 *Ibid.*, 69, 63.

40 *Ibid.*, 53-54.

41 *The Breach Repaired in God's Worship: or, Singing of Psalms, Hymns, and Spiritual Songs, proved to be an Holy Ordinance of Jesus Christ* (London: 1691), 99, 176. For a more extensive analysis of Keach's argument than is possible here, see especially Vaughn, "Public Worship and Practical Theology",172-187.

42 *Breach Repaired*, 21.

43 "Benjamin Keach and Nonconformist Hymnology", 79.

44 *Breach Repaired*, 62-64.

45 *Ibid.*, 105-106, 110.

46 *Ibid.*, 139-141.

47 *Ibid.*, 74, 80-81.

48 *Ibid.*, 93-94. On this issue, see further Clifford, "Benjamin Keach and Nonconformist Hymnology", 82-84; Vaughn, "Public Worship and Practical Theology", 183-184.

49 Vaughn, "Public Worship and Practical Theology", 155-157, 162. For studies of his hymns, see *ibid.*, 143-162; Music, "Hymns of Benjamin Keach".

50 For a recent history of these Seventh-day Baptists, as well as other Sabbatarian groups in England during the seventeenth and eighteenth centuries, see Bryan W. Ball, *The Seventh-day Men: Sabbatarians and Sabbatarianism in England and Wales, 1600-1800* (Oxford: Clarendon Press, 1994).

51 *Ibid.*, 122-123. Hannah eventually joined the Quakers.

Conclusion

1 W. M. S. West, "Baptists and Statements of Faith" in Cyril S. Rodd, ed., *Foundation Documents of the Faith* (Edinburgh: T. & T. Clark, Ltd., 1987), 88-97.

2 *Ibid.*, 87, 88.

3 For this phrase, I am indebted to a remark made by C. H. Spurgeon and quoted by David Kingdon, "C H Spurgeon and the Downgrade Controversy" in his *et al. A Marvellous Ministry. How the All-round Ministry of C H Spurgeon Speaks to Us Today* (Ligonier, Pennsylvania: Soli Deo Gloria Publications, 1993), 128. See also the attitude of the American Baptist James P. Boyce in this regard: Thomas J. Nettles, "Creedalism, Confessionalism, and the Baptist Faith and Message" in Robison B. James, ed., *The Unfettered Word: Southern Baptists Confront the Authority–Inerrancy Question* (Waco, Texas: Word Books, 1987), 150. In Boyce's opinion, confessions of faith serve as a "protection of the spirituality of the church and simplicity that is in Christ".

4 In this regard, see the discussions by Robert Paul Martin, "Introduction: The legitimacy and use of confessions" in Samuel E. Waldron, *A modern exposition of the 1689 Baptist Confession of Faith* (Darlington, Co. Durham: Evangelical Press, 1989), 9-23; Erroll Hulse, "The 1689

Confession - its history and role today" in his *et al.*, *Our Baptist Heritage* (Leeds: Reformation Today Trust, 1993), 28-31.

5 *The Glory of a True Church, and its Discipline display'd* (London: 1697), 63-68, *passim*.

6 "Independency and Interdependency" in *Our Baptist Heritage*, 37. This article is an excellent discussion of the significance of seventeenth-century Baptist ecclesiology for Calvinistic Baptists today.

7 A goodly number of seventeenth-century Baptists also used church covenants as part of the process whereby new members were admitted to the local church. See Charles W. Deweese, *Baptist Church Covenants* (Nashville, Tennessee: Broadman Press, 1990), 24-38.

8 *Modern exposition*, 430.